Life World Library
Life Nature Library
Time Reading Program
The Life History of the United States
Life Science Library
Great Ages of Man
Time-Life Library of Art
Time-Life Library of America
Foods of the World
This Fabulous Century
Life Library of Photography
The Time-Life Encyclopedia of Gardening
The American Wilderness
Family Library
   The Time-Life Book of Family Finance
   The Time-Life Family Legal Guide

LIFE LIBRARY OF PHOTOGRAPHY

Travel Photography

BY THE EDITORS OF TIME-LIFE BOOKS

TIME-LIFE BOOKS, NEW YORK

ON THE COVER: In confronting such works of ancient and modern man as the Acropolis and the Eiffel Tower, the travel photographer has a problem: how to keep his picture from looking like everybody else's. Alfred Eisenstaedt (in Athens) and René Groebli (in Paris) met that challenge. Focusing on two of the most photographed monuments in the world, they put their own highly personal stamps on scenes that clearly say travel.

Contents

*Portions of this book were written by Robin Jones.
Valuable aid was provided by Charles E. Rotkin
and by these individuals and departments of Time
Inc.: Editorial Production, Norman Airey, Nicholas
Costino Jr.; Library, Peter Draz; Picture
Collection, Doris O'Neil; TIME-LIFE News
Service, Murray J. Gart; Correspondents Margot
Hapgood (London), Maria Vincenza Aloisi and
Josephine du Brusle (Paris), Elisabeth Kraemer
(Bonn), Ann Natanson (Rome), Martha Green and
Patricia Newman (San Francisco), Frank Iwama
(Tokyo), Mary Johnson (Stockholm), Robert
Kroon (Geneva), Tomas A. Loyaza (Lima),
Richard Oulahan (Madrid), James Shepherd
(New Delhi), Strobe Talbott (Belgrade), Ann
Turner (Nairobi), Leslie Ward (Los Angeles).*

All too often the traveling photographer, looking at his tour pictures back home, finds that the fond memories he had hoped to preserve on film have faded as rapidly as a winter vacationer's tan. He wishes he had been better at capturing that atmosphere, at evoking whatever it was that made the visited place so captivating at the time—in short, at bringing the travel experience back alive. The purpose of this volume is to help him do that.

The traveler with the camera faces some special obstacles he does not have to cope with at home. He cannot carry as much equipment. He spends a great deal of time getting to his destination and an equal amount of time getting back. He may be frustrated by the fleeting opportunity, particularly when it is complicated by bad weather.

Yet he can pack a single camera bag with equipment sufficient to cover nearly any situation he will encounter. He can take some excellent pictures en route, from plane, train or car. And, most of all, once he fully comprehends the sense of the place, he can learn how to communicate that sense fully in his photographs.

Usually the feeling of place and atmosphere is best conveyed by color. Most traveling photographers tend to think in terms of color; there are 97 color photographs in this volume. Yet a black-and-white picture often expresses more of the traveler's sensations than color can, and pages 109-128 show how professional photographers have used monochrome to advantage.

The chapters in this book combine the advice of professionals with examples from their travels, and offer their tips on everything from what to take along and how to handle lighting problems in dark church interiors to what times of day to take certain pictures, and even how to turn bad weather into an asset. How well that advice can be applied is shown by the fact that 20 of the pictures included are by amateurs.

The Editors

CARL MYDANS: *Sunset at Moorea, Tahiti*, 1971

An Expert's Advice to the Tourist-Photographer

Carl Mydans, a LIFE staff photographer since the magazine's first issue, here draws on 35 years of experience in traveling with a camera to offer practical advice on taking pictures away from home that will be memorable photographs long after the trip is over.

One day when I first traveled to New York, I suddenly glimpsed a wondrous spectacle: through the fiery, backlit cables of the Brooklyn Bridge a sunset transformed the city into a glowing mirage. Slowly it grew into a colossal Stonehenge, drenched in red. My hands trembling, I ran this way and that, looking through my finder, trying to catch in my camera what had caught in my heart. As I write this—four decades and hundreds of thousands of negatives and transparencies later—with my traveling case packed with fresh film and my cameras checked anew, my spirits are rising as they do whenever I set out on another trip. For ever since that vision in New York, I hope for another such sight wherever I go, one that will set my hands trembling as I raise my camera. I have found them often enough to make traveling—with camera—the most satisfying activity in my life.

Most people seem to feel the same way. We travel not just to be on the move, but to take pictures along the way. It is not hard to understand why, for pictures of travels allow us to relive our experiences. Looking at the image of a famous view that seemed thrilling when it was first seen rekindles that thrill; when we study the picture of the unexpected street happening that offered a sudden insight into a country, we recall our pleased surprise all over again; even when we see ourselves or our traveling companions trapped in some problem with luggage or language, we enjoy in retrospect what seemed at the time an awkward plight.

Each traveler's record of his trip is a personal expression, catching the flavor and drama of his own experiences. No two people see things exactly alike, and however many are standing together clicking away at the same subject, their pictures will all be different. Millions have photographed Mount Fuji and the Eiffel Tower, but I have never seen precisely duplicated pictures of either one. Just as that unique view of a phantom New York was waiting for me on the Brooklyn Bridge many years ago, such a picture-moment may be waiting anywhere for anyone. To be ever hopeful of coming upon it is the thrill of traveling with a camera.

Because I have been traveling for years and pictures have been the heart of my journeys, friends leaving for a trip frequently ask me what to photograph and what cameras and lenses to use. Be assured that expensive equipment is not necessary; an outfit that provides flexibility at home, such as the one shown on page 79, will do so away from home.

Much more important than the equipment is the photographer's familiarity with it. Know the capabilities of lenses and film, and avoid buying anything new just before setting off. The temptation to get a brand-new camera or extra lens to take on a trip may be almost irresistible, but unless the new equipment has been tested at home, the results are likely to be frustrating. A woman I met recently in Thailand came to me near tears because, although she had thought she understood everything about her new camera, she could not remove the exposed film and reload it. After she shot one roll, she missed the pictures that came later on a tour through Bangkok and the countryside—and they were some of the best opportunities of her trip.

It is also wise to decide before leaving home how black-and-white pictures will be handled. Most travelers shoot only in color, and that is generally a mistake because some scenes come across best in monochrome. Yet using both types of film raises a problem of its own; each calls for a different artistic approach, and the process of thinking out pictures is different. It is surprising how photographic capability is impaired by switching back and forth from one to the other. When a couple travels together, one might decide to shoot color, the other black and white. The decision might be made on the basis of differences in taste; on pages 109-128, for example, there are some travel photographs that are better for having been taken in black and white. Even color film alone can pose a difficult choice: in some locations, a mixture of daylight and artificial light may raise the question of whether to use tungsten or daylight film. Do not worry about it; shoot whatever is in the camera at the time. The result may not be exactly true color but usually the difference will be so slight that everyone will be delighted with the pictures.

The most important advice I can give on equipment has nothing to do with the technicalities of emulsions or optics. It is simply: Carry a camera at all times. The rule applies from the beginning of a trip to its end, for many memorable pictures can be made en route—at terminals, aboard planes, ships, cars and trains. It is not commonly realized that train travel in particular provides excellent opportunities to take exceptional photographs. Trains usually ride higher than the areas they pass through and the view from them is often commanding, surpassing what can be photographed from ground level. Pictures taken from trains provide a kaleidoscope of scenes: countryside and city, homes and factories. Not only are there open views of fields, rivers and mountains, but there are also chances to look behind the scenes, to photograph the backyards—the underside of a country's life that might be missed traveling by the plane that lands at the airport in the city's outskirts or the automobile that follows the scenic highway into the center of town.

Shooting from a moving train may seem impossible to the traveler. Actually it only takes a little practice and is a fine game of anticipation. At first the fleeting, imperceptible delay between what the eye sees and the finger snaps may result in some surprises: the green Malaysian rice field may come out a blurred bridge railing; and the Thai temple blinking in the sun may turn into an embankment of weeds. But it takes only a little practice to learn to anticipate and, even in such brief moments, to select. Do select, however; snapping away feverishly will only waste film.

The injunction to keep a camera at hand applies more forcefully at the trip's destination. Remember that it is a mistake to leave the camera in the hotel on rainy or overcast days; frequently weather can add an extra element of mood or atmosphere to the picture. And remember especially that a scene worth photographing is seldom the same when returned to later. Often it is not there at all, so it should be photographed at this opportune moment. Other scenes may improve as they change—with changing light or weather —in which case patience will bring even greater rewards. I recall once taking pictures on the Tahitian island of Moorea, where the afterglow of sunset colors the sky and the sea with incredibly beautiful reds and oranges. Having chosen my area for a picture, I returned every evening at sunset. But sometimes clouds obscured the sun, while at other times the sea was empty. Then one evening all the components came together: the sky and clouds were tinged with those gorgeous colors, the afterglow spread across the sea, and at that moment two Polynesian women in a dugout paddled into the scene. In that instant I had the photograph I had been hoping for *(page 11)*.

Glorious panoramas can be found almost everywhere, and one way to locate them is to buy picture postcards. Local photographers may not have the best sense of composition; but they have scouted the area for years, and their selection of positions can provide a quick choice of prospects. In fact, a postcard picture can provide a challenge as well. The traveler with a sharp eye and a keen imagination can get considerable satisfaction out of taking an even better picture. Some striking examples are on pages 204-222.

I think it is a mistake, however, to concentrate only on the panoramas. The small things in a scene are often equally interesting. A texture-rich close-up of a weathered fence or of the eroded bricks in an old wall might highlight the character of a country or say something crucial about its culture. Details are equally important in pictures of people. The bent body of the old peasant stooping in the doorway might be no more dramatic than a close-up of his gnarled hands. The picture of the cobbler working at his dusty bench might also call for a look at such details as the shoe he is making, the odd-shaped tools lying in the leather scraps on the ground, or even the worn sandals on his own feet. Such a sequence—what the professional photographer calls "taking the scene apart," or "the one-two-three"—often can tell far more about the subject than any one picture.

People are an essential ingredient in travel pictures, for they can impart at least as much local flavor as a photograph of a place; and often they provide the personal excitement that the visitor wants most to preserve on film. There are two approaches to photographing people: that of the "invisible witness," who waits for his subjects to compose themselves into a picture he feels is right, and that of the photographer-director, who takes charge of his subjects and moves them around until he has them composed the way he wants them. Most travelers use the first approach to catch informal glimpses of street life and market scenes, but even in those situations it is sometimes wise to ask people if they will let themselves be photographed—especially if the photographer senses that they are becoming suspicious or resentful.

Anyone who has ever had this request made of him will have an idea of their reaction: perhaps embarrassment, amusement, annoyance, or occasionally a feeling of obligation to international goodwill. In Japan it is not uncommon for an American to be asked to join a group of Japanese tourists standing stiffly in front of a giant Buddha while their companion takes a picture of his friends and the strange-looking *gaijin* in their midst. I have been in this situation a number of times myself, and I know the feeling of the interminable wait while the smile grows wooden on my face.

In front of a camera most people are stiff and self-conscious unless the photographer can provide the spirit to enliven them. Putting some life into their actions and expressions can be accomplished even among foreigners who speak a strange language. Enthusiasm and good nature are a universal language; surprisingly often, people will do their best to respond.

Sometimes, however, even the most engaging spirit is not enough to relax subjects. The simpler a people's society, and indeed the more eager they are to accommodate a stranger, the more rigid they may become before the camera. Some people still seem to believe that if they twitch a muscle they will ruin the picture. I have found that one way of getting around this natural tendency to freeze up is to snap the posed picture and then, lowering my camera, to thank my subjects warmly for their kindness. They almost always thank me in return. It is at this transient moment, when they are relaxed and smiling, that I take the picture that shows them as they truly are.

It is necessary to remember, however, that there are many people who, for deeply personal reasons, object to having their picture taken. To try to force such people is not only futile but unkind. Some object to being photographed because they are ashamed of their clothes or surroundings, some because of religious taboos or even because they are convinced that a copied image of themselves might be invaded by evil spirits. Once while I was taking pictures of a Chinese shopkeeper and his wife in Djakarta, their daughter suddenly stepped in to be photographed between them. Instantly the mother flew out of the picture. "No! No!" she protested. "If you photograph three people together, one of them will soon die!"

At other times the reasons are more pragmatic. Once in Yugoslavia I stopped to take a picture of a group of farmers pitching hay by the roadside. The men had their trousers tucked into high boots and the women wore kerchiefs on their heads and bright-colored skirts. A bottle of wine stood by the cart wheel, and the mood was festive. As I approached, one of the women waved me off angrily, and when I stopped, perplexed, she walked away. The others laughed. "Her husband doesn't know she's here," they explained.

It is important to proceed carefully on occasions like this when people show a reluctance to be photographed, for the camera does at times invade privacy, and accordingly the burden of good manners is on the photographer. Chapter 6 has further suggestions for getting enjoyable pictures of people—enjoyable to the subjects as well as the visitor.

Courtesy in choosing subjects for pictures may not suffice in some lands, however. While tourists with cameras are now welcomed nearly everywhere, their reception can chill quickly when they focus on certain kinds of subject matter. In some places, particularly in the countries of Eastern Europe, the unwarned traveler may not always recognize the scenes that it might be imprudent to photograph. From my own experience, I would say that it is best to avoid the following subjects in those regions: all queues, because the authorities in these countries are sensitive about publicizing any shortages of consumer goods; all military institutions and installations; seaports; railroad junctions; all views from airplanes; views from heights in industrial cities (in military parlance known as "bomb-folder pictures" because they are the kinds of pictures bombardiers use to identify targets); drunks (I learned to make it clear that I was not using my camera when I saw one coming); slums or any other subject that might reflect social problems and therefore be deemed embarrassing to national pride. I was once detained for taking pictures of an ancient church that had been blown into dramatic tatters by years of storm and neglect. (For a detailed list of restricted subject matter, country by country, see pages 84-87.)

Elsewhere I have found few restrictions other than those concerning military installations, which are common in most countries. However, one foreigner who was recently allowed to travel to North Korea tells the following story: accompanied by a guide, he took some pictures of a slum in Pyongyang and left the exposed film cartridge in his room. After he returned home and had the film developed, he found that his exposed roll had been replaced with another. This one showed nothing but monuments.

Such incidents are blessedly rare, for photographic restrictions have disappeared almost completely in recent years. Nowhere is the change more dramatic than in Japan. There, before World War II, a visitor's cameras were most often taken from him or sealed; when he was allowed to use them, he was watched while taking pictures and was required to have his film developed and to clear the negatives with a censor before he could leave. Today, of course, there are no longer any such restrictions, and the country is overrun with people using cameras, Japanese as well as visitors.

The new freedom to photograph wherever and whenever there is a good picture in turn presents a challenge to the traveler. In all the variety of permissible subject matter, what should be taken? The best answer is not a new one: The greatest pleasure comes from pictures of things that suit the photographer's own personal interest. The student of history might seek out ancient locations evocative of great events—the haunted rooms of Holyrood Palace in Edinburgh, the crumbling ruins along the old Appian Way in Rome, the fields of Waterloo in Belgium. An art lover might concentrate on the frescoes inside Romanesque cathedrals, a gourmet on early-morning market places or on the restaurants that serve memorable food. I know of one traveler who photographed every meal he ate on his trip; I know another who for years has taken pictures of every hotel room he stayed in.

I once had an English professor who said that when he traveled he studied —of all things—apples and cheeses. They took him everywhere, and transformed him from an idle voyager into a man with a mission. It was this special interest, he said, that made him a citizen of the world, a member of every society he visited. I pass his example on as my most important advice on traveling with a camera: the traveler with a camera should plan his trip around whatever constitutes his own particular apples and cheeses. *Carl Mydans* □

The Traveler's Eye

The qualities that make a good travel photographer are also those that make a good traveler: curiosity about the infinite variety in the world around him, appreciation for other cultures, and an eye for scenes that are unusual, telling or incongruous. The best way to develop such qualities is, apparently, to travel. Few of us can fully appreciate the visual possibilities in our own environment: our eyes become so attuned to their usual diet of sights that a remarkable candelabralike tree across the street or an amusing confrontation between a long-haired neighborhood child and a shaggy dog goes unnoticed —or, if noticed, goes unphotographed.

But once we assume the role of traveler—whether to distant lands or the nearest state park—our senses seem sharper and our perceptions clearer. These faculties can be heightened by practice even on short jaunts. And they are worth developing, for they make the difference between static, cliché pictures destined to languish in a drawer and those that vividly recall the experiences and sensations of travel.

While the vivid picture cannot often be grabbed on the run it is well worth stalking. When you arrive at a new place take a leisurely walk around, or a tour-bus ride, with camera in hand, of course, in case something strikes your eye, but not with any feeling that you *must* get pictures now. At this point it is reconnaissance that you care about. Pay close attention to what is happening, and make written or mental notes about what ideas to follow up. The bustle at a construction site, the dickering at a produce market, the bottlenecking of traffic at a bus intersection, even the way local people use a park or playground—let nothing escape your eye. Then when you return for picture taking you will have a good idea where the action is and what vantage points you want to pick—so as to get not any old picture, but a memorable one.

The photographers represented on the following pages, all but a few of whom are amateurs, had two things in common as they traveled: they kept their cameras loaded and their eyes wide open. None of the pictures was posed or contrived; all the situations were there for the photographer to observe or even, as in the case of the picture at right, to anticipate. What makes each unique is that the photographer recognized some extraordinary quality in the scene that would forever recall some aspect of his trip—whether it be the strange juxtaposition of Indian tepees on a campground at Pendleton, Oregon *(pages 24-25),* the incongruity of two massive moving vans afloat on the Grand Canal in Venice *(page 27),* or the humor in a conservative Englishman's reaction to an unconservative miniskirt in London *(page 33).*

The ability to spot unfolding picture possibilities and the patience to wait for them to develop paid off for one photographer-tourist in a picture that unmistakably conveys the U.S.S.R. today. The photographer, visiting Leningrad just prior to its annual October Revolution celebration, noticed preparations being made to erect a huge painted image of Lenin. Though he was on hand the next day when the crane arrived, he had to wait almost all day before there came a moment when the lighting was right, the composition interesting —and Lenin's figure rose proudly above his city.

JULES ZALON: *Lenin*, 1971

The crazy tilt of an English pillar box adds a note of whimsey to an otherwise commonplace street scene in Greenwich. The photographer came across the precariously balanced mailbox unexpectedly, and deliberately exaggerated its leaning-tower appearance by using a wide-angle lens and shooting from an extremely low angle.

There is no scarcity of delightful half-timbered ▶ Tudor houses to photograph in England. But there cannot be many that look as amusingly tipsy as these. The fact is that these houses, though four centuries old, are still remarkably sturdy and livable. Modernizing them with perfectly squared-off doors and windows has only served to accentuate the casual construction typical of 16th Century homes—and to help the viewer realize where and when the picture was taken.

PATRICK THURSTON: *Pillar Box*, 1968

BILL BINZEN: *East Anglian House*, 1970

JOHN DORISS: *Singapore Hearse*, 1965

◄ Not everyone comes across a hearse on his travels and, of those who do, few choose to photograph it. Yet the amateur photographer who noticed this gaudy, flower-bedecked hearse while wandering through Singapore's back streets was so impressed by the visual interest of the Chinese characters, the proud display of the deceased's portrait and the almost-joyful total effect that he seized the opportunity to get a picture of an unusual custom in a strange city.

Few foreigners traveling in Spain venture onto the local buses that rumble from town to town. But anyone who does—like Robert Tschirky—never forgets the experience. He spent some time talking to the farmers who were loading a bus with their belongings—including a newly purchased fat pink pig—at the end of a market day. Once they got used to the photographer's presence, they lost their self-consciousness and he was able to get a remarkably evocative glimpse of street life.

L. ROBERT TSCHIRKY: *Tarazona*, 1964

23

As dusk settled along the Umatilla River in Pendleton, Oregon, Dan Budnik photographed this improbable scene of Indian tepees pitched near a camping area, with the lights of camper trucks and town-dwellers' homes in the background. The occasion for this uniquely American oddity was the annual Pendleton Roundup, part rodeo, part carnival, which brings Cayuse, Umatilla and Walla Walla families from their reservations to dance, camp out in their tepees, show off their feathered headdresses, and otherwise act out their ancestral customs for photographers and other visiting palefaces.

DAN BUDNIK: *Tepees along the Umatilla River*, 1969

ELIOT ELISOFON: *Hong Kong Harbor*, 1962

*Surrounded by picturesque old junks in the
middle of Hong Kong Harbor, LIFE photographer
Eliot Elisofon noted the garish incongruity of
Western advertising signs punctuating the high-
rising façade of the Oriental city. Instead
of eliminating the signs from the picture, he
actually made use of these intrusive notes
to heighten the anachronistic charm of the junks.*

MARJORIE HARLEY: *Moving Day on the Grand Canal*, Venice, 1964

Sometimes a photographer can make up a lost chance: Marjorie Harley, passing an elegant Venetian palazzo on the Grand Canal, was enchanted by the building's frescoes. Unhappily, her camera was back at the hotel. So the next day, camera in hand, she returned, to find it was moving day. Although this was not the picture she had intended, it illuminates life in a canal city.

27

Where but in a park would the camera be likely to find such a treat as the vibrant color of London shopgirls assembled on bicycles for a parade? Parks seem to encourage the unusual and spontaneous, and they may be the ideal place to exercise the traveler's eye, as these four pictures made by freelance Patrick Ward demonstrate.

In these pictures the photographer concentrated on the Serpentine, a lovely lake in Hyde Park's sylvan setting only steps away from the bustle of London. Among the scenes that caught his eye —perhaps because of their incongruity as London sights—are a proper Englishman (above left), complete with his bowler, briefcase and umbrella, walking past bathers' tents; the placid determination of a father and son (left), fishing in the rain under an umbrella draped with plastic; and the fine carefree abandon of an early-morning swimmer making an unself-conscious dive.

MARY LEATHERBEE: *Balloon Seller in Chapultepec Park,* 1968

Sundays in Mexico City mean Chapultepec Park,
and Chapultepec Park means balloons. Nearly as
many glistening balloons swing through the park
as children, and the brightly colored round
shapes are an out-of-the-ordinary reminder of
local custom. To capture on film this memory of a
Mexican Sunday, the photographer had to arrive
early one overcast morning, before the balloon
vendors were sold out of their floating stock.

JADWIGA IRENA DANIEC: *Weighing Station in Kiev*, 1971

If no one in calorie-conscious Kiev is going to use this shiny white scale, who can blame its attendant for taking his ease in the shade of his umbrella? This amusing vignette was shot on the run: the photographer had just time enough to focus and snap the picture before her tour moved on. Throughout the trip she had kept her camera set at f/8 and 1/125 second; fortunately, as here, the light was consistently good.

RHODA SIDNEY: *The Well*, Mérida, 1971

By itself, the cast-bronze public well in the small
town of Mérida has little to recommend it. But it
does take on new interest when photographed as
a center of Spanish life. Here, the photographer
noticed a workman who was more intrigued by the
housewives in hair curlers than by his own chore.

Girl watching reached a new high in London in ►
the era of the miniskirt, and all of the elements
in the picture at right speak of that moment
in time. Against a background of pub and racy old
touring car, a sobersided Englishman stares
at an unconcerned advertisement for the style.

GREGORY SHUKER: *Chelsea*, 1967

The garden of a villa overlooking Lake Como
—enclosed by stately plane trees and including a
pool afloat with water lilies—makes an enchanted
setting. And it is given a surrealistic touch by the
use of a wide-angle lens and low shooting angle.
Together they emphasize the pool and bring
the background statue into a position that makes
it seem to be climbing the stairs to the garden.

MAITLAND A. EDEY: *Villa Balbianello*, Lake Como, 1965

The First Pictures from Afar **2**

93. J.J.a. on Donkey El Kab.

PHOTOGRAPHER UNKNOWN: *Tourists and a Donkey at the Ruins at El-Kâb*, Egypt, c. 1890

A Planet Fresh for the Camera

In the middle of the 19th Century, the world was still full of unexplored wonders, but steamships and railroads were making it possible for people to reach more and more of them. And the camera was a magic box that helped those who traveled to preserve and spread their vision—enabling those who did not travel to look at all the far-off marvels without ever leaving their firesides. The photograph itself was no less a marvel than the wonders it depicted. "Oh, infinite volumes of poems that I treasure in this small library of glass and pasteboard!" exclaimed Oliver Wendell Holmes of his collection of three-dimensional stereographic photographs. With it, he wrote, "I stroll through Rhenish vineyards, I sit under Roman arches, I walk the streets of once-buried cities, I look into the chasms of Alpine glaciers, and on the rush of wasteful cataracts. I pass, in a moment, from the banks of the Charles to the ford of the Jordan."

The travel photographer of the day did more than provide pleasant daydreams for Holmes and other stay-at-homes. He acquainted them with the flora and fauna, the art and architecture of lands that most of them would never see for themselves. He showed them how other peoples lived, worshiped, dressed and fed themselves, amused themselves, married, gave birth and died—some according to customs that already were vanishing forever, like those of the American Indians. In European cities the photographer recorded the crumbling of old landmarks; on the American frontier he recorded the breaking of new soil.

Travel pictures exerted much of their great influence on the public mind through an institution called the illustrated lecture, a slide show (glass slides, in black and white) of photographs of distant places projected in schools, churches and homes. One William H. Rau of Philadelphia advertised that his slides were "made on specially imported thin crystal glass of a superior quality, entirely free from bubbles." Single slides sold for 50 cents; a set of 60 that took the viewer on a "Tour of the World" could be had for $30, complete "with descriptive reading, packed in grooved box." The tour started out with a view of the interior of Independence Hall in Philadelphia, proceeded west across the United States through Yellowstone, Yosemite and San Francisco, then moved on to China and Japan, through the Middle East and Europe, ending back at the Statue of Liberty in New York.

The public illustrated lectures became a lucrative business for educationally oriented showmen, who compiled their own slide collections and talks to go with them. One of the most famous was an engaging youth named Burton Holmes (not related to Oliver Wendell Holmes), who had so much fun with his venture that he called it his "plan for dodging work"; in fact, he worked hard putting together a very good show indeed. For his first performance —given on a fall day in 1893 at 11 a.m. because he could rent the hall for a bargain price in the morning—he used pictures he had previously taken on a trip to Japan, and wrote and memorized material to go with them. When Holmes' second show began that same evening the house was full to overflowing with Chicago's high society, all in evening dress, and Holmes was launched on a lucrative career that was to make his name a household word.

Most of the early travel slides, like travel pictures of all kinds, were made not by the men who used them but by professional photographers. The pioneers among them were an intrepid breed, each one a man of parts: adventurer, explorer, artist, teacher and bearer of wondrous tales.

He also had to be a craftsman and a technician. No push-button camera holding a lightweight roll of plastic film existed for the early traveling photographer, and no obliging laboratory stood ready to process his pictures for a fee; he had to know how to do everything, from composing and focusing and exposing the picture to sensitizing the plate and developing it. Moreover, until the perfection of the dry-plate process in the 1870s, he had to do all the necessary operations on the spot, because development could not wait. That meant hauling cartloads of equipment weighing up to 120 pounds all the way to the scene: two or three cameras as big as some television sets; as many as 100 glass plates for negatives, some as large as 20 x 24; a variety of lenses and tripods for each of the cameras; a tent to set up as a darkroom; jugs of chemicals and an assortment of incidental gear.

So burdened, the first photographers contented themselves with recording the look of the land—the cool serenity of the Parthenon, the virgin plains and towering mountains beyond the Mississippi. As the land and landmarks became more familiar and as photographic equipment became less cumbersome, photographers looked more closely at the people they encountered in their travels: visions of human beings smoking opium in Persia, having their toenails cut in China or dancing in a plea for rain in the Arizona Territory were no less astonishing than views of ancient monuments.

Toward the close of the 19th Century, travel pictures changed as advances in transportation attracted a whole new class of travelers and an indefatigable inventor named George Eastman devised a mass-produced roll-film camera (page 60), fathering a whole new breed of photographer. The new travelers, touring farther and farther afield with their easy-to-use cameras, began not only to snap spectacular landscapes and exotic people, but to record their own presence—to photograph and to be photographed in faraway places, making pictures to show and tell about when they got home. An art that previously had been limited to a hardy and well-heeled elite now was ready to pass into the hands of anyone with imagination and a few dollars to spare. Travel pictures became more casual, more spontaneous —each individual's own interpretation of what he saw. □

Documenting the Wonders of the World

Nowadays, when a flight from Paris to Athens takes a couple of hours, and the steps of a journey on the moon's surface can be followed minute by minute on TV, it is difficult to re-create either the wonder or the apprehension inspired by travel hardly a century ago.

In 1849, when the future novelist Gustave Flaubert took leave of his mother to join photographer Maxime Du Camp *(page 44)* on a picture-taking expedition to the Middle East, the event caused a family crisis. "What a cry she uttered when I shut the door of the living room," Flaubert wrote. "It reminded me of the one I heard her make when my father died." The young man was hardly more composed himself, and Du Camp found him later the same evening prostrate before the fireplace, sobbing: "I'll never see my homeland again."

Not all travelers were as fearful as Madame Flaubert and her son, but there was reason for misgiving. Only a few foreign sites were as serene as the Acropolis *(right),* and the first photographers who ventured on tour to bring stay-at-homes their first clear views of strange lands and even stranger people found rigors aplenty. John Thomson, an unexcitable Briton who took his camera to China, wrote of "placing my revolver beneath my pillow, and the matches close to the candle." Timothy H. O'Sullivan, who covered much of the American frontier, wrote of the "unlimited number of the most voracious and particularly poisonous mosquitoes" he encountered, not to ignore "that most enervating of all fevers, known as the 'mountain ail.' " Charles R. Savage, another photographer of the American West, noted that every campsite had to post guards "to keep a sharp lookout for any sneaking red-skins."

Other photographers found ways to make friends with the strange people they met, although winning over the natives took an elastic turn of mind. Edward S. Curtis, who photographed the Hopi maidens on page 55, had to learn and abide by Indian customs before he was made privy to their secret rituals. "I fasted with the Hopis," he wrote, "wore the costume of a priest, painted my body in the sacred manner and slept in the kiva beside a native priest who was my informant and interpreter. Since I was a novitiate, the snakes were placed around my neck before going into the bags."

Not that snakes and deserts, glaciers and savages appeared on every 19th Century travel photographer's itinerary; some faced hazards no worse than the gondola traffic in Venice or the street traffic in Paris, both slow moving. But by the time these far-ranging recorders of the exotic were finished, the world was no longer quite the mystery it had been; some of its grandest sights were on the way to becoming clichés.

With the almost unreal sharpness of detail that ▶ Renaissance landscape painters had favored, a 19th Century traveling photographer recorded the ruined majesty of the Acropolis, half a mile distant from his camera, in the brilliance of the Greek sunshine. Another camera, its focusing hood draped over it, is set up to capture the same stunning scene from a different point of view.

PHOTOGRAPHER UNKNOWN: *The Acropolis from Philopappos, Greece, c. 1870*

Venice, with its network of romantic canals and its suggestion of Oriental exotica, had great appeal for Victorian travelers and stay-at-homes alike. In this picture Stieglitz, who had gone to Germany to study engineering and instead took up photography, summarized the fabled city in a vignette of dappled water and crumbling masonry.

ALFRED STIEGLITZ: *Venice*, 1897

MAXIME DU CAMP: *The Sphinx and Pyramids, Egypt, 1851*

*The face of the Great Sphinx at Giza, which few
people had then seen, looms up ahead of a row of
pyramids in one of 125 pictures made for the
French Ministry of Education and published in the
first book to be illustrated with photographs.*

FRANCIS FRITH: *Great Wall of China,* c. 1860

*In a faraway land that, in the 19th Century, drew
traders and missionaries before it attracted
tourists and archeologists, a British photographer
demonstrates the vast scale of the Great Wall of
China by placing three companions in his picture.*

ALFRED STIEGLITZ: *Paris*, 1894

46

At the junction of Boulevard des Capucines and
Rue Scribe—the Old England store stands
on the corner at left—Paris goes about its business
heedless of the photographer, the pedestrians
and horse-drawn carriages moving along
the glistening street on a rainy day in 1894. This
deceptively casual approach, showing the
everyday appearance of a seemingly exotic city,
was revolutionary in the 1890s, when most
travel photographs focused on the monumental.

A year before Yellowstone was set aside as federal property—and long before any but explorers had set eyes on it—photographer William Henry Jackson made the first pictures taken in that Wyoming wilderness. The picture at right shows Thomas Moran, official painter to the expedition, surrounded by volcanic rock and pools of boiling water. It was such stunning photographs by Jackson that persuaded a dubious Congress to designate the 3,578-square-mile tract a national park, the first in the world.

235. MAMMOTH HOT SPR'S THE ROSTRUM

WILLIAM HENRY JACKSON: *Mammoth Hot Springs*, Yellowstone Park, 1871

49

FÉLIX BONFILS: *Pilgrims in Bethlehem*, c. 1850

A French photographer caught thousands of
pilgrims milling about a hill in Bethlehem
on Christmas Day, fulfilling their dreams of
commemorating the nativity of Christ in the place
of His birth. Until about the time the picture was
made, this dream of devout Western Europeans
had been realized only by the most adventurous.
But the development of the steamship in the
middle of the 19th Century greatly simplified travel
to the Middle East, where religious feeling
and wanderlust attracted many to the Holy Land.

The Holy Land also drew travelers with scholarly
interest in its historical background. At right a
German photographer documented the Church of
the Holy Sepulcher in Jerusalem, traditional
site of Christ's entombment, catching in this small
close-up the spare lines of the architecture,
the parched stones that bespeak centuries of
baking in the sun, and the poignant presence
of a human pilgrim suggested by the abandoned
basket lying in front of the sealed doorway.

AUGUSTE SALZMANN: *The Holy Sepulcher*, Jerusalem, 1856

Climbing Mont Blanc in the French Alps is still a big adventure; the ascent in the 1860s, laden with photographic gear, was something new and all but incredible. Yet Louis Auguste Bisson, who had studied under Daguerre, and Louis' brother Auguste Rosalie did just that on an expedition commissioned by Emperor Napoleon III. One member of the team got this view of the heavily laden climbers inching their way up the mountain. At 16,000 feet the below-zero temperatures nearly froze the wet-collodion emulsion, which had to be applied to the plates just before use.

BISSON FRÈRES: *Mont Blanc*, 1860

Focusing on the Human Race

ARTHUR FELDMAN: *Apache Squaws and Babies*, Arizona, c. 1890

By the 1860s, travel photographers had expanded their interests from landscapes and architecture and begun to concentrate on the people they found. Increasingly sophisticated equipment made it possible to record subjects that breathed and shifted about—and were ultimately *(Chapter 6)* to become a major part of travel photography.

For Europeans this new approach usually meant examining Africans and Asians in their native environments; for Americans it usually meant documenting the Indians of the West, who often seemed more alien and exotic than any people on earth. Some observers found them simply objects of curiosity; a few were farsighted and sensitive enough to perceive that the Indians' fading culture should be captured in pictures before it disappeared altogether. Two photographers possessed of such perspicacity were Arthur Feldman and Edward S. Curtis, who made the pictures on these pages. These two men gave Easterners a measure of insight into the pride and dignity of their strange Western countrymen, who until then had most often been portrayed only as stereotypes of savagery.

◄ Some Apache mothers and their babies sit for a traveling photographer with a white child mysteriously present—probably a member of a family working among the Indians. Except for the factory-made doll in the outsider's lap, the artifacts—the bowl and the basket, the long skirts and the loose-fitting blouses—all show the beauty and craftsmanship of Apache culture.

Four Hopi girls gather on a pueblo terrace in Walpi Village, their centuries-old dwelling place, composing themselves in a timeless travel picture. Their hairdos, coiled to resemble squash blossoms, are a sign they are marriageable.

EDWARD S. CURTIS: *Hopi Girls*, Arizona, c. 1900

At an open-air barbershop, four Egyptians made up a scene that, to 19th Century European viewers, seemed a candid glimpse of the exotic Orient. Inside the arcade under the intricately carved mushrabiya (wooden latticework), a customer reclines to have his head shaved while a boy stands behind with a fan to cool him; outside, a man (possibly waiting his turn) smokes a yard-long water pipe and another boy sits in silent meditation.

The picture of Persian textile craftsmen at ▶ right, like many of the best of the early travel photographs, was made by a man engaged primarily in nonphotographic work. It was taken by a German engineer who, while constructing the first telegraph line across the country, gathered a priceless store of photographs documenting Persian society of the day. This one shows a group of cotton washers demonstrating one of the many steps needed to produce cotton prints. The cotton washers, well paid and middle class, had one of the largest guilds in Persia.

PHOTOGRAPHER UNKNOWN: *Egyptian Barbershop,* c. 1880

ERNST HÖLTZER: *Persian Cotton Washers*, Isfahan, c. 1882

JOHN THOMSON: *On a Chinese Junk*, Hankow, 1871

With a lordly mien that shows his importance, the photographer's Chinese interpreter takes an imperial stance in front of the cook and an attendant on the Yangtze riverboat that carried them from Hankow. Not every Chinese modeled so cheerfully. "The superstitious influences," Thomson wrote, "rendered me a frequent object of mistrust, and led to my being stoned and roughly handled on more occasions than one."

A traveling chiropodist from Peking removes a ▶ corn and pares the toenails of a client somewhere in rural China as another customer waits his turn. Pictures like these, which were meant to convey "the arts, usages and manners which prevail in different parts of the Empire," were Thomson's goal, sure to please the curious back home.

JOHN THOMSON: *Chinese Chiropodist*, c. 1870

The Tourist Gets into the Scene

For about half a century, travelers who practiced photography were for the most part professionals; the rest were amateurs who devoted so much time and expense to its techniques, and acquired so much skill, that they qualified as semipros. The subjects favored by both in far-off places were the strangest they could find—at first the strange-looking landscapes and architecture, then strange-looking people engaged in strange occupations.

Later in the 19th Century, photographers changed and their subjects did, too. Thanks to easier travel and freer-flowing money, tourists increased in number and traveled ever farther—and when they got where they were going, they became the camera's targets. As equipment became faster and less obtrusive, the photographs became more candid and the subjects loosened up —sometimes to the point of being unaware they were being photographed at all *(page 67)*. More typically, travelers asked that their pictures be taken,

to show to friends at home and to remind themselves of what they had seen and done. A professional photographer was as likely as not to be on the spot to oblige. Often he was the local entrepreneur who stood ready to record the eager visitors clambering up the sides of pyramids, lolling in frilly litters borne by porters, or mugging in a row before ancient pillars. He posted himself at the site, importuned the tourists as they arrived, and then sold them their pictures for a nominal fee.

But the biggest change in travel photography occurred when George Eastman *(opposite)* invented the Kodak box camera, a gadget so easy to use that anyone could work it. Now when tourists went traveling, they could do the picture-taking themselves. "You press the button; we do the rest," said Eastman in advertising his brain child, and he meant it. He even thought to include a notebook with each roll of film, so the photographer could identify his pictures when he got them back.

People who traveled switched very promptly to recording their experiences on film instead of in journals. One tourist took a Kodak with him on an around-the-world bicycle trip; on one of Lieutenant Robert E. Peary's expeditions in search of the North Pole in 1898, a Kodak went along on a dog sled to document the event. The travelers with cameras still had to keep their wits about them, however; President Grover Cleveland was said to have spent all day on a fishing trip taking pictures, only to discover that he had forgotten to wind the film between exposures.

Most of the old-time traveling photographers were not so absent-minded. They left a legacy of pictures that are charming, interesting and irreplaceable as a record of a world now largely lost. Some were taken by professionals with complex equipment; some were taken by the new legion of amateurs with Eastman's handy Kodak; but all show the new dimension that photography added to travel.

George Eastman, who put the Kodak box camera ▶ on the market and thereby put photography into everybody's hands, stands aboard the S. S. Gallia in the act of working his new invention. The picture was taken by a friend of Eastman's with another of the recently introduced No. 2 Kodaks.

FRED CHURCH: *George Eastman with a Kodak*, 1890

For a good many years before George Eastman sent tourists on their way with handy cameras they could use for making snapshots of their own *(preceding pages),* earlier entrepreneurs had been supplying them with another kind of photographic reminder of the trips they made away from home. That was the stereograph image, a pair of pictures (almost but not exactly alike) that, when looked at through a stereoscope, appeared to be three dimensional. These photographs, which were introduced about 1840, became in time the Victorian equivalent of the color slides that are sold at souvenir stands the world over today. They could be bought for a few cents, either on the scene or at an emporium back home.

The view might be a picture of anything anywhere, but for a long time the most popular subjects were the sites that were luring vacationing travelers —places that were historic like the Acropolis *(near right above),* exotic like Tangier *(far right above),* or very adventurous like the Matterhorn and Yosemite *(bottom).* Many views, like these, had tourists in them, suggesting to the purchaser that in just such scenes he might find himself. On the backs of some were short lessons with such information as: "Mountain climbing is an interesting sport, even though it is dangerous. Most of the tall peaks of the world have been climbed by hardy men. Each year there is a death toll, due to carelessness or accident; but this does not cause the sport to cease."

17130—Teeming Arab Life in the Market Place, Tangier, Morocco.

Nearly a Mile Straight Down, and only a Step, Yosemite, from Glacier Point, California, U.S.A.
Copyright, 1901, by Strohmeyer & Wyman.

PHOTOGRAPHER UNKNOWN: *Ruth at Thebes*, c. 1890

Striking a demure pose that was to be repeated in countless tourist snapshots, a camera-carrying girl traveling in Egypt arranged herself by the stone head of Ramses II, while a companion immortalized the scene on the round frame that marks it as an early Kodak picture. The photographer is unknown, but the handwritten note in the album from which this picture came indicates that the girl's name was Ruth.

Equally informal, but more likely to have been recorded by a professional photographer using a large view camera, a group of tourists—one of them astride a camel and several carrying parasols against the blazing sun—gather outside the court of Amenhotep III at the Temple of Luxor.

PHOTOGRAPHER UNKNOWN: *The Nile Party*, c. 1888

PAUL MARTIN: *Bathing at St. Helier, Jersey, 1893*

Three jolly Englishmen on holiday by the sea send some cheerful waves in the photographer's direction. Paul Martin was a pioneer of informal pictures, taking full advantage of a newly developed small and unobtrusive type of camera that had a built-in plate-changing device for making several shots in rapid sequence. Through his camera, he wrote, "I discovered the joy of reacting spontaneously to real life. . . ."

A well-dressed couple, happily cuddling in the sand far from home, remain apparently as oblivious to the photographer as they are to the vacationers in the background. The sneaked picture was made possible by Martin's inventiveness. When he was not traveling in search of candid scenes he tinkered with his camera, and one of his inventions was a silencer that reduced the startling clunk of the plate-changing mechanism to an unobtrusive click.

PAUL MARTIN: *Spooning by the Sea, Yarmouth, 1892*

PHOTOGRAPHER UNKNOWN: *The Williamson Family Rocking the Boat, Colorado, c. 1892*

Gimmick shots had great appeal in the Gay
Nineties, when life was carefree and the camera
was the traveler's new toy. Here a traveling family
has some sport with a strange geological
formation, called the Boat Rock, that they found
near Turret, Colorado—now a ghost town.

For all the fun and games to be had on tour, travel ►
also required stamina and sturdy legs. These
tourists proved it for the folks at home by getting
the photographer to record them clambering
up a corner of the Great Pyramid at Giza, with
only their parasols and each other for support.

G. LEKEGIAN: *Egypt*, c. 1888

Even where the going seemed rough, a camera was at hand to record a well-heeled tourist like this one, a British gentleman traveling the easy way through the mountains of Madeira. While his companion looks on, he reclines in a litter borne by two porters wearing the white uniforms and straw hats that mark their occupation.

PHOTOGRAPHER UNKNOWN: *Madeiran Wayside*, c. 1885

71

PHOTOGRAPHER UNKNOWN: *Bicycling through Europe,* 1894

*Travelers quickly took up the newly popular
bicycle in the late 19th Century, and these hardy
cyclists paused for a snapshot in Europe, their
flags showing they are Americans far from home.*

The Well-Planned Trip 3

ED EDWIN: *Sunlight in the Air, Late Afternoon,* 1967

What to Take Along

The traveler who photographs has a double packing job to do. Once the choice of drip-dry clothing, shoes and toilet articles is dealt with, he turns to assembling his photographic gear. This is a more exacting task: it involves planning a kit that is light enough to be carried by hand, sturdy enough to withstand the jolts of transportation and varied enough to deal with nearly any picture that may present itself. The photographer does not want to be burdened with equipment he will never use, but he does want to be prepared for the unexpected picture and to be able to do it justice. What does he take along, and what does he decide to leave behind? Individual requirements necessarily vary, but a suggested set of useful equipment is shown on page 79. Special equipment and a traveling case are illustrated on pages 80-81.

There is mental packing to do, too. For the traveler should learn the regulations and customs of countries on the itinerary—nations, like people, have their idiosyncrasies. Many impose no official limits on the equipment that can be taken into them; others have rigid restrictions *(charts, pages 85-87)*. All have some rules about what can be photographed within their countries. French customs officials admit tripods; does the Louvre do the same? Yes, for a small fee. The government of Spain puts no specific limit on photographic equipment allowed into the country, but can the equipment be taken inside Madrid's famous museum, the Prado? No, not even a camera. On the other hand, in many churches and cathedrals there are no restrictions except the obvious one of common courtesy; the photographer's opportunities, as Dmitri Kessel shows on pages 98-106, are vast. For a museum-by-museum rundown, see the charts on pages 96-97.

Once the photographer has learned what he will be allowed and has decided what he will need in the way of cameras, lenses and other appurtenances, he faces another decision: should he take it all along when he leaves home or get some of it en route? The answer is simple: with the single exception of film, it is not a good idea to pick up basic photographic equipment abroad for use on the trip. One good reason is that United States Customs allows the traveler to bring only $100 worth of duty-free goods back into the country. Anything valued at more than that amount is subject to customs duty; and that can substantially raise the price of a bargain lens.

More important than saving money is saving time; travel days are too precious to spend practicing with unfamiliar gear. All equipment should have a thorough trial run to be sure it works, and to make its use as familiar as winding a wristwatch. Many pictures call for all the manual dexterity the photographer can command, and that requires familiarity with the equipment. Also, if anything is out of order it should be discovered in advance.

How much film the traveler needs depends on his photographic intentions; most serious amateurs average about three rolls for each day of travel. Film is the one thing that can easily be found and safely purchased in every major city. It costs more abroad than it does in the United States, but it may be necessary to buy it there. Some countries limit the amount of film that can be brought in: Italy and New Zealand, for example, allow only five rolls. (Details on film restrictions are also included in the charts on pages 86-87.)

In any country the photographer may suddenly find that he does not have the right film in his camera for a chosen subject. He need not give up on the picture: even if he has nothing but a roll of daylight film with him, he can still get that shot of a museum interior. The trick is to "push" the film—that is, set the exposure as if the film's ASA rating were double or quadruple its actual value (the effect is underexposure by one or two f-stops); then instruct a custom processing laboratory to compensate for the underexposure by prolonging the duration of the developing period. For example: using a daylight film with an ASA rating of 100 in a dark interior, set the exposure meter for ASA 200 or 400. Then adjust f-stop and shutter speed as the meter indicates (it will now register as if the camera contained ASA 200 or 400 film). Expose the entire roll in this way; do not switch the ASA setting in mid-roll. Mark instructions on the roll (on adhesive or masking tape) when it is removed. "P1" or "P2" is useful shorthand that the processing technician will understand; it means that he is to push one or two stops in developing. A custom developer (not the corner drugstore) will treat the film accordingly—for a slight extra charge—and the chances of success are good.

Whatever a photographer takes in the way of gear, he should be sure to carry it personally and not check it with his luggage. (An exception: a tripod that telescopes handily will fit in any good-sized suitcase.) One reason for carrying everything is to cut down the risks of theft and damage en route. But more important, a camera in a suitcase cannot be used, and subject matter is to be found on every step of a journey. Mary Leatherbee caught the image of snow reflections on the wing of an airliner in Alaska because her camera was beside her and loaded when she noticed the phenomenon *(page 91)*. All sorts of scenes can be shot when traveling by automobile, often without even getting out of the car; Victor Landweber imaginatively framed an Arizona sunset in his windshield *(page 90)*. With the camera handy and the traveler's eye open, anyone can do the same, from the moment he shuts the front door behind him and starts his travels to the moment he gets back home. □

The Basic Equipment

Choosing photographic equipment for a trip means striking a delicate balance: too much and mobility is hampered, too little and the picture of a lifetime may be missed. The kit at right is flexible for the traveler, yet weighs only 8½ pounds. At its heart is a 35mm single-lens reflex camera (1) with a normal lens. Small, sturdy, with quick and simple through-the-lens focusing, this type is a practical choice for the traveler. Two extra lenses—a 35mm wide-angle lens (4) and a 135mm long lens (5)—broaden the range of pictures that can be made.

A second camera body (2), useful in case of breakdown, can carry a second type of film for quick switching from dim interior pictures to bright street scenes, or from color to black and white. It should take the same lenses and accessories as the main body.

Travel increases the risk of damage to delicate gear, requiring lens caps (6), body caps (one is shown on the extra body) and lens cases (7). Extra neck straps (3) are handy if the destination is a hot or damp location where leather may rot rapidly (some photographers prefer rot-proof metal straps). A cable release (8), with a spare for insurance, is indispensable for steady, long exposures. Plastic kitchen bags (13) protect equipment in dusty or rainy weather, but some dust is inevitable, and lens tissue (12) should be carried.

A combination incident-light and reflected-light meter (9) is useful when a built-in camera meter might be misleading—gauging exposure for a bright scene framed in a dark doorway, for example—and it also serves as a check on the camera meter. Batteries can be hard to find; carry at least one spare.

As for filters, a skylight/haze filter (10) and a polarizing filter (11) are most useful, but filters are so compact that more can be carried easily.

Many a tripod that is light enough to carry with ease may prove too flimsy to stand steady. A miniature tripod (18) can be a better choice; it can be placed on a car fender or a church pillar *(page 94)*. A ball-jointed tripod head (17) sets the camera at any angle on the tripod.

An electronic-flash unit (14) is essential for interior or nighttime photographs. This one, about the size of a cigarette pack, couples to a recharger (15) that adapts to foreign currents.

Circumstance determines how much film (16) to carry. For a trip around Europe or the United States it makes sense to buy film as needed; for a journey to the jungles of Borneo the traveler must stock up in advance.

1 | 35mm SLR camera with 55mm (normal) lens and hood
2 | spare SLR body and body cap
3 | neck straps
4 | 35mm (wide-angle) lens and hood
5 | 135mm (long) lens and hood
6 | lens caps
7 | lens cases
8 | cable releases
9 | incident-reflected light meter and extra battery
10 | skylight/haze filter
11 | polarizing filter
12 | lens tissue
13 | plastic bags
14 | flash unit
15 | house-current adapter for strobe
16 | film
17 | ball-joint tripod head
18 | miniature tripod

Special Equipment and a Shockproof Case

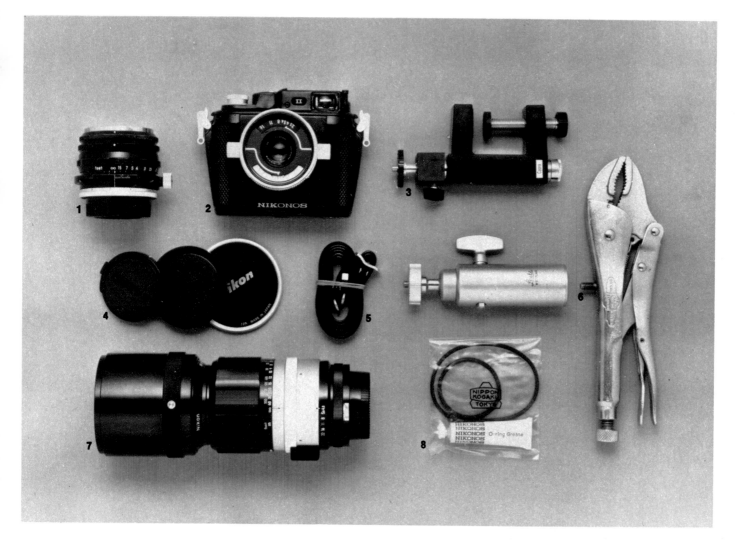

1 | **P-C (distortion-correcting) lens**

2 | **underwater camera with 35mm (normal) lens**

3 | **camera clamp**

4 | **lens caps**

5 | **spare neck strap**

6 | **vise-grip camera clamp to fit ball-jointed tripod head**

7 | **300mm lens**

8 | **extra gaskets and lubricant for camera**

Besides the basic equipment that nearly any traveler will find useful, some specialized extras prove their worth for photographers who are fascinated by particular kinds of pictures. Among the most popular of these individual photographic interests are architecture, nature and underwater subjects, and for each there are relatively simple accessories that will more than repay the cost of buying them and the trouble of bringing them along on the trip.

The architecture enthusiast is faced with the special problem of distortion introduced when the camera is tilted to take in a tall structure: vertical lines run together so that the building seems to be leaning back. The solution is a P-C,

or perspective-correction, lens (1). It can be shifted—up, down or sideways —relative to the camera so that it brings in a full view of a building while the camera is held level; there is then little distortion of the image.

The architectural photographer also finds a clamp (3) useful where a tripod is forbidden—as it is in many museums.

A very handy homemade clamp can be rigged from a vise-grip wrench (6), which holds tightly to such rounded objects as posts and rails; simply drill the wrench handle to take a tripod screw and fasten on a tilting tripod head.

For underwater photography, a watertight SLR (2), shown with its rubber neck strap (5), weighs little and is mod-

estly priced; extra lens caps (4) as well as gaskets and lubricant (8) should be taken along. A long lens is a must for animal photographers; the 300mm lens (7) can be handled easily.

To ensure a safe trip for valuable photographic equipment, carry it in an aluminum case (right) lined with foam plastic cut to fit each camera and lens.

What Extra Lenses Can Do

The photographs of three London monuments at right—all familiar targets of travelers' cameras—demonstrate what the right lens can do to make a better picture, and emphasize the lesson by showing what happens when a wrong lens is used. The photographer used the same 35mm camera and remained at one position for each series of pictures, shooting first with a 35mm wide-angle lens, then with a 55mm normal and then with a 135mm long lens.

The pictures of St. Paul's Cathedral *(top row)* were taken from a sidewalk at one side, where a full, sweeping view was possible. The wide-angle lens *(left-hand picture),* giving a generous lateral coverage of about 63°, was able to provide a good general view; it encompassed all the façade and got the dome in the picture as well. The normal 55mm lens *(center picture)* could not adequately capture the great building; it lost the lantern and spire and some of the surrounding structures. In the picture at far right a 135mm lens so drastically reduced the width covered that only the lantern and spire appear; it fails as a comprehensive picture of St. Paul's although it might be considered an interesting detail photograph.

Although the wide-angle lens proved a good choice for the view of St. Paul's, the long-distance shot of Tower Bridge *(middle row)* required the normal lens. The camera was about one quarter mile away and the first attempt, with the wide-angle lens, proves disappointing; the expanse shown is so broad that the picture tells the viewer more than he wants to know about the dreary architecture on either side of the bridge, while the bridge itself is reduced in importance. But the normal lens gives a nice flavor of river life. Attempting the photo with the long lens results in a confused, almost unrecognizable picture without any point of emphasis.

When the Tower of London was photographed from the far side of the Thames *(bottom row),* the long lens came into its own. The wide-angle shot got a great expanse of river, but an insignificant panorama of trees with a building half-hidden in the trees. With the normal lens there is still too much river and landscape, and the tower remains annoyingly small. The third picture, taken with the long lens, causes the tower to fill more of the frame, leaving just a suggestion of its setting —enough to give a sense of locale.

wide-angle lens

wide-angle lens

wide-angle lens

normal lens

long lens

normal lens

long lens

normal lens

long lens

Rules and Regulations in Foreign Lands

Since World War II a remarkable thing has happened in the field of travel: the freedom to move about among the nations of the world—and to photograph—has become almost universal. Even in many countries that not long ago were sealed off behind the Iron or Bamboo Curtain, the tourist and his cameras are now welcome. What is more, the restrictions that remain on camera use are generally no more stringent than those the traveler takes for granted in America—where he assumes as a matter of course that neither he nor his cameras will be allowed inside a Minuteman silo or Fort Knox.

The limitations vary somewhat from country to country, and it is wise to learn in advance what equipment or subject matter might cause problems. It also makes sense to investigate provisions for processing film and for supplying power for flash equipment. The charts opposite and on the following pages can serve as a guide, but rules change from time to time, and the traveler who plans on out-of-the-ordinary photographs should check in advance with the nearest consulate of the country he plans to visit.

The most common restrictions involve subject matter. As might be expected, almost every country (including the United States) prohibits indiscriminate photographing of its military sites, and many limit taking pictures from private planes. But some countries have taboos that are not so predictable. The Dominican Republic, which is sensitive about poverty, prohibits photographing slums and beggars; Haiti, at the other end of the same island, says nothing about the poor but frowns on taking pictures of the National Palace. Swit-

zerland bans all photographs of the interiors of its celebrated banks. Iceland forbids taking pictures of four endangered species of birds (so they will not be frightened away from their mating and nesting areas). In Argentina and France the taboo involves cemeteries (evidently a matter of respecting the privacy of the dead); in China, entrances to the Peking subway (because the subway platforms also serve as bomb shelters).

With his photographic equipment the tourist is on fairly safe ground; every country assumes that he will carry cameras. But customs officials may take a traveler laden with more than three cameras, or with heavy-duty tripods, for a professional—and tax his equipment accordingly. Some countries, mainly those in Eastern Europe, require that a visitor register all equipment and film on arrival; if that happens to you, be careful not to discard either the registration slip or any equipment, for if an item is missing on departure a duty may be charged. Some countries require a tax or a refundable bond on equipment exceeding a specified limit; a few may demand the surrender of excess gear on arrival, to be returned on departure (be sure to get a receipt).

Film processing abroad varies so much in speed and quality that the safest procedure is to keep undeveloped film for the return home or else send it to a United States laboratory in a mailer that shows the processing was paid for when the film was bought. Be sure to mark the package *"photographic film —do not X-ray";* imported goods are often X-rayed to detect contraband, and X-rays fog film.

How long exposed film can safely be

kept undeveloped depends partly on climate. In the cool air of Scandinavia a couple of months will make no difference; in the heat of North Africa image quality begins to deteriorate almost immediately. But in some areas, government regulations can be a determining factor. The U.S.S.R. and some Eastern European nations restrict the importing of negatives, exposed film and photographs, so before entering any of these countries mail home whatever was shot earlier in the trip.

The vagaries of electric power outside the United States may trouble the traveler who expects to recharge his electronic-flash unit. Throughout Europe and in most parts of Africa and the Middle and Far East, electrical voltage is double the 110 or so used in the United States, the frequency is different (50 cycles instead of 60) and wall sockets vary as well. If you visit Greenland bear in mind that it is one of the few places left in the world that uses DC instead of AC. Most countries in the Americas, however, follow United States practice. An adapter will solve most of your electrical problems.

The last leg of the trip is not always clear sailing, for equipment purchased abroad may be subject to United States customs duty. To avoid trouble with gear that looks as if it might have been bought outside the United States (a foreign-made camera, for example), carry some evidence—a sales slip or an insurance policy—to prove that it was bought before the trip and that any required taxes were paid on it. Better yet, register equipment before leaving, by taking it into the United States Customs Office at the airport at least two hours before departure time.

The Americas	customs limitations on traveler's gear		limitations on subject matter					local color processing	local electric power
country	still cameras and accessories per person	film rolls per camera	military and border areas	airports, seaports, railroad stations	views from commercial planes	views from private planes	other restricted subjects[1]	time required in days	volts/cycles
Argentina	3 different	no limit set	permit req.	permit req.	permit req.	permit req.	cemeteries	2-5	220/50-60
Bahamas	2 (register)	no limit set	permit req.	no limit	no limit	permit req.		1-3[2]	110-125/60
Barbados	no limit set	no limit set	no limit	no limit	no limit	no limit		slow	110/50
Bolivia	no limit set	no limit set	permit req.	no limit	no limit	no limit		2-3	220/60 (La Paz: 110/60)
Brazil	1	no limit set	no limit	no limit	no limit	no limit		2-3[3]	110/60
British W. Indies	no limit set	no limit set	permit req.	no limit	no limit	no limit	U.S. Naval Base	1-6[3]	110/60
Canada	no limit set	no limit set	no limit	no limit	no limit	no limit		2-7	110/60
Chile	no limit set (register)	no limit set	forbidden	no limit	no limit	no limit		3-5[3]	220/50
Colombia	no limit set	no limit set	permit req.	no limit	no limit	permit req.		3-5	110/60
Dominican Republic	no limit set	no limit set	permit req.	no limit	no limit	no limit	slums, beggars	slow	110/60
French W. Indies	no limit set	no limit set	no limit	no limit	no limit	no limit		slow	110/60
Greenland	no limit set	no limit set	forbidden	no limit	no limit	permit req.		no color	220-DC
Guatemala	no limit set	no limit set	permit req.	no limit	no limit	no limit		slow	110/60
Haiti	no limit set	no limit set	permit req.	no limit	no limit	no limit	National Palace	slow	110/60
Jamaica	no limit set	no limit set	no limit	no limit	no limit	no limit	slums, beggars	slow	110/60
Mexico	1	12	no limit	no limit	no limit	permit req.	archeological sites	3-14	120/50-60
Netherlands W. Indies	no limit set	no limit set	no limit	no limit	no limit	no limit		slow	110/60
Panama	no limit set	no limit set	permit req.	no limit	no limit	permit req.		slow	110/60
Peru	no limit set	no limit set	permit req.	no limit	no limit	permit req.		2-3[3]	220/60
Venezuela	no limit set	no limit set	forbidden	no limit	no limit	permit req.	guarded areas, refineries	2-3[3]	110/60

[1] Most of the subjects listed in this column are forbidden; a few, however, may be photographed with special permission. Check locally.

[2] Processing is available for prints only, not for slides.

[3] No Kodachrome processing is available.

Europe	customs limitations on traveler's gear		limitations on subject matter					local color processing	local electric power
country	still cameras and accessories per person	film rolls per camera	military and border areas	airports, seaports, railroad stations	views from commercial planes	views from private planes	other restricted subjects[1]	time required in days	volts/cycles
Austria	2 (register)	no limit set	permit req.	no limit	permit req.	permit req.		3-10	220/50
Belgium	2	no limit set	permit req.	no limit	no limit	permit req.		5-7	110-220/50
Czechoslovakia	no limit set (register)	no limit set	forbidden	forbidden	permit req.	permit req.	bridges, government buildings	slow	220/50
Denmark	2	no limit set	permit req.	no limit	no limit	permit req.		4-5	220/50
Finland	no limit set	no limit set	forbidden	no limit	no limit	permit req.		2-7[3]	220/50
France	2	no limit set	permit req.	no limit	no limit	permit req.	cemeteries	5-7	110-220/50
East Germany	no limit set (register)	no limit set	forbidden	forbidden	forbidden	forbidden	bridges, R.R. junctions, military personnel	slow	220/50
West Germany	no limit set	no limit set	permit req.	no limit	permit req.	permit req.		1-3	220/50
Great Britain	no limit set	no limit set	permit req.	no limit	no limit	no limit		3-10	240/50
Greece	no limit set	no limit set	forbidden	no limit	no limit	permit req.		4-7[3]	220/50
Hungary	no limit set (register)	no limit set	forbidden	permit req.	permit req.	permit req.		3-14[3]	220/50
Iceland	2	no limit set	forbidden	no limit	no limit	no limit	birds[2]	2-3[3]	220/50
Ireland	no limit set	no limit set	permit req.	no limit	no limit	no limit		2-10	220/50
Italy	1	5	forbidden	permit req.	permit req.	permit req.		3-8	120-220/50
Luxembourg	no limit set	no limit set	permit req.	no limit	no limit	permit req.		2-7	220/50
Netherlands	2	10	permit req.	no limit	no limit	forbidden		2-5	220/50
Norway	no limit set	no limit set	forbidden	no limit	no limit	permit req.		1-3	220/50
Poland	2 (register)	12	forbidden	forbidden	permit req.	permit req.	bridges, factories	3-20	220/50
Portugal	no limit set	no limit set	permit req.	no limit	no limit	no limit		2-5	220/50
Spain	no limit set	no limit set	permit req.	no limit	no limit	no limit		2-5	220/50
Sweden	no limit set	no limit set	forbidden	permit req.	permit req.	permit req.	factories	2-5	220/50
Switzerland	no limit set	no limit set	permit req.	no limit	no limit	no limit	bank interiors	3-7	220/50
U. S. S. R.	1	no limit set	forbidden	forbidden	forbidden	forbidden	bridges, R.R. junctions, factories, military personnel	slow[3]	220/50
Yugoslavia	no limit set (register)	no limit set	forbidden	forbidden	permit req.	permit req.		14-21	220/50

[1] *Most of the subjects listed in this column are forbidden; a few, however, may be photographed with special permission. Check locally.*

[2] *Iceland prohibits the photography of some endangered species of birds at their nests.*

[3] *No Kodachrome processing is available.*

Africa, Middle East and Far East	customs limitations on traveler's gear		limitations on subject matter					local color processing	local electric power
country	still cameras and accessories per person	film rolls per camera	military and border areas	airports, seaports, railroad stations	views from commercial planes	views from private planes	other restricted subjects[1]	time required in days	volts/cycles
Algeria	2	5	permit req.	permit req.	permit req.	permit req.	inside mosques	no color	120/50
Australia	2	no limit set	permit req.	no limit	no limit	no limit		3-7	220/50
Ceylon	1 (register)	10	forbidden	no limit	forbidden	forbidden	bridges, beggars	7-28[2]	220/50
China	no limit set (register)	no limit set	forbidden	forbidden	forbidden	forbidden	bridges, R.R. junctions, factories, subway entrances	4-8[2]	110-230/50
India	1 (register)	10	forbidden	no limit	forbidden	forbidden	bridges, beggars	7-21	220/50
Indonesia	no limit set	no limit set	forbidden	permit req.	no limit	no limit		2-5	110-220/50
Iran	no limit set	no limit set	forbidden	no limit	no limit	permit req.		2-7	220/50
Iraq	no limit set (register)	no limit set (register)	forbidden	forbidden	permit req.	permit req.	women, inside mosques	no color	220/50
Israel	no limit set	no limit set	forbidden	permit req	forbidden	permit req.	some sects[3]	2-3[2]	220/50
Japan	no limit set	no limit set	permit req.	no limit	no limit	no limit		1-3	110/60
Jordan	1 (register)	no limit set	forbidden	no limit	no limit	permit req.		no color	220/50
Kenya	1 (register)	1 per week (renewable)	forbidden	no limit	no limit	permit req.	parliament, guarded areas, some tribes[3]	1-3[2]	220/50
Lebanon	no limit set	no limit set	forbidden	no limit	no limit	no limit		2-5	110/50
Morocco	no limit set	no limit set	permit req.	no limit	permit req.	permit req.	royal palace	4-5[2]	110-220/50
New Zealand	2	5	permit req.	no limit	no limit	no limit		1-10	220/50
Philippines	no limit set (register)	no limit set (register)	forbidden	no limit	no limit	permit req.		slow	220/50
Republic of S. Africa	no limit set (register)	no limit set	forbidden	no limit	no limit	permit req.	prisons, R.R. lines	1-3	220/50
Rhodesia	no limit set	no limit set	forbidden	permit req.	permit req.	permit req.	factories	1-3	220/50
Saudi Arabia	no limit set (register)	no limit set (register)	forbidden	permit req.	permit req.	permit req.	native dress	no color	220/50
Tahiti	2 different	5	forbidden	no limit	no limit	no limit		3-5[2]	110-220/60
Taiwan	1	6	forbidden	permit req.	permit req.	permit req.	bridges	2-5[2]	110/60
Turkey	2 (register)	5	forbidden	no limit	no limit	permit req.		7-14[2]	220/50
United Arab Republic	no limit set (register)	no limit set (register)	forbidden	forbidden	forbidden	forbidden	factories, oil lines, guarded areas	1-10[4]	220/50

[1] Most of the subjects listed in this column are forbidden; a few, however, may be photographed with special permission. Check locally.

[2] No Kodachrome processing is available.

[3] Some groups refuse to be photographed for religious reasons. Check locally.

[4] Processing is available for prints only, not for slides.

Photographing en Route

ALFRED EISENSTAEDT: *Twentieth Century Limited,* 1952

All too often, people begin to shoot their travel pictures only after they have arrived at their destination. But getting there is half the fun, as the Cunard steamship ads used to say; the journey presents opportunities for good pictures, like the bridge scene opposite, that appear en route. Many help introduce a travel sequence: the frontispiece of this chapter *(page 75),* Ed Edwin's picture of golden afternoon sunlight sparkling from the wing of a plane, could be the title frame of a slide show, setting the tone for a record of joyous adventure. Edwin, a freelance, always carries a loaded camera in the air: "Some of your best views are available up there," he says.

Airplanes give unparalleled overall views, while cars, boats and trains are good bases from which to capture unusual shots of the world flashing by. But picturemaking from any moving vehicle requires special care. To minimize window reflections, try to sit on the shady side and hold the camera parallel to the glass. Never steady the camera against the vehicle, because vibration will be transmitted to blur the shot; instead brace your arms against your body, which will absorb the shaking.

Yet motion may be the effect desired, as in the picture above, which Alfred Eisenstaedt made, not from a speeding train, but of it. The viewer reads the blur as a symbol of speed.

LENNART OLSON: *Bridge at Tjörn, Sweden, 1961*

◄ *The train had just begun to move when this picture was made late on a summer evening. Fading light required a long time exposure that blurred the image, capturing the powerful surge of one of the last American luxury trains as it streaked away on its journey to New York.*

The curving sweep of a bridge was photographed in morning light with black-and-white film, which emphasized linear form to make an abstract composition. Man-made designs of this sort present themselves to the traveler along almost any highway—striking but easily missed subjects.

VICTOR LANDWEBER: *Arizona Sunset,* 1971

*Using his truck's windshield to frame a desert
sunset, the photographer snapped a unique,
dramatic view from an Arizona highway. The
cloud bank and the top of the windshield march
together in a tandem diagonal; what seems to be
a grotesquely twisted giant cactus is really a
metal bracket of the right-hand rearview mirror.*

MARY LEATHERBEE: *Reflections in an Airplane Wing*, the Alaska Range, 1965

*Flying near Mount McKinley in a commercial
plane, LIFE senior editor Mary Leatherbee saw
snowfields and peaks mirrored on the underside
of the wing—and got this doubled picture
because she always travels with a camera at
the ready. Her 35mm wide-angle lens helped keep
both the wing and the land below in focus.*

91

The Well-Planned Trip: Photographing en Route

The brave little sailboat at upper right puts in scale this vast aerial seascape of the Atlantic washing against the shore of Cape Cod. The billowing light areas are sand bars, rinsed by a foot or so of ocean water. This picture was made from 2,500 feet on a special photographic flight just as the plane banked on its approach from Monomoy to Chatham, but the low-altitude short hops of local airlines provide traveling photographers many opportunities for such shots.

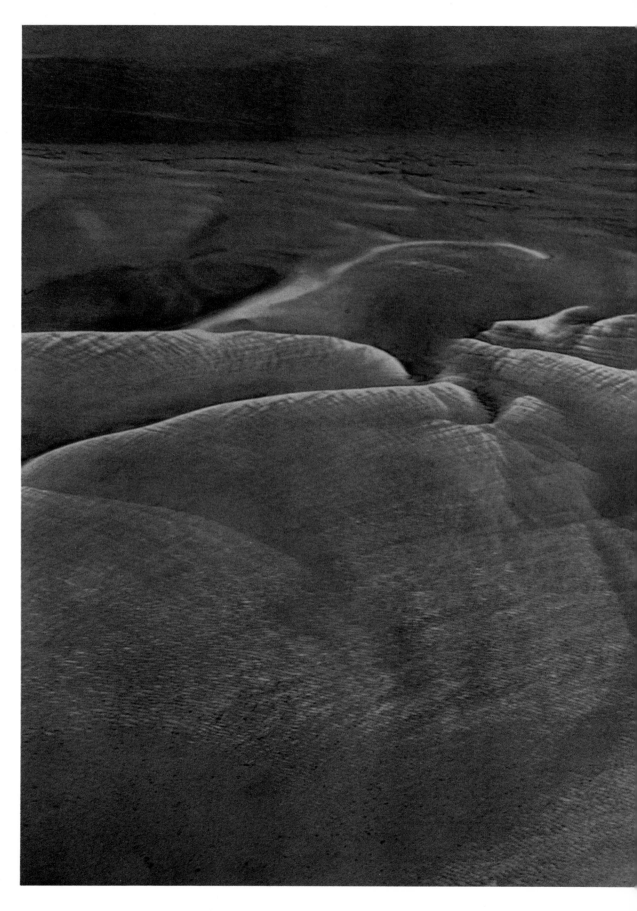

WILLIAM GARNETT: *Over Cape Cod between Chatham and Monomoy Island,* 1966

Working with Works of Art

One of the main reasons for dragging extra equipment along on plane and train trips is the great wealth of art that can be photographed on arrival—famous sculpture and paintings, magnificent cathedrals, massive monuments. No traveler wants to miss them, and the pictures he gets will be much better if he has a few accessories. While professionals like Dmitri Kessel, noted for his cathedral views *(following pages),* generally use lavish kits of complex gear, the limited extras listed on pages 80-81 can make excellent results possible, as shown by the pictures here, shot with 35mm cameras inside museums.

The most useful lenses besides the normal 50 or 55mm are those of moderately long and moderately short focal length—for a 35mm camera, a 135mm long lens and a 35mm or 28mm short lens. They enable the photographer to get close-ups and interesting aspects of objects that would be difficult to catch with a normal lens. They also permit positioning the camera to exclude people who might clutter the view.

A long lens, however, may worsen another photographic problem in museums and cathedrals: the light in them is often too limited to permit shutter speeds fast enough to avoid blurring with a hand-held camera, and the long lens is not only slower than a normal one but its magnifying effect also magnifies camera shake. The usual solutions—flash to increase the light or a tripod to steady the camera—may be forbidden. In such a situation, a miniature tripod *(right)* can be handy. Alternatively it is often possible to hold the camera firmly against a wall or railing or even, in some cases *(opposite),* to simply place it flat on the floor.

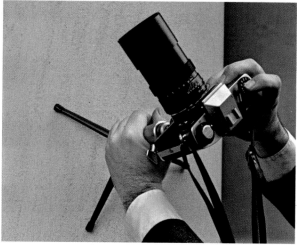

An overall view of Michelangelo's David in Florence *(above)* was taken with a hand-held 35mm SLR and a 50mm lens. A shutter speed of 1/30 second recorded some movement among people in the picture. For the close-up, a 135mm lens was used and stopped down to f/11 to gain depth of field. This small aperture necessitated a shutter speed of ⅛ second—so slow the camera required a solid mount. It was set on a miniature tripod with a ball-and-socket head and then held against a column at one side of the statue *(right).*

JOHN PORTER: *Ceiling in the Salone of the Barberini Palace,* 1969

A 17th Century ceiling painted by Pietro de Cortona in Rome's baroque Barberini Palace was photographed with a 35mm rangefinder camera and a wide-angle lens. The photographer focused from a position close to the floor, then placed the camera on its back in the center of the floor and tripped the shutter with a cable release.

Museum Rules on Photography

One of the traveling photographer's greatest opportunities is to take his own photographs of the masterpieces of art preserved in museums. Many tourists let this chance slide because they think art museums are off limits to photographers. How wrong they are can be seen by glancing at the charts on these pages. Of the 46 American and foreign treasure houses of art that are listed, only six—none in the United States—bar the traveler's hand-held camera. Three in the United States place no limit on his use of flash and many, at least under certain conditions, go so far as to admit his tripod. Even in the U.S.S.R., according to Intourist, the government travel agency, it is possible to make personal photographs of the country's huge collections of masterpieces; a permit is required but it is not hard to come by.

Every museum does impose some restrictions, and for good reason. All seek to protect their collections from deteriorating, and repeated use of flash can cause the colors in oil paintings and tapestries to fade—two Italian museums allow flash to be used on sculpture but not on other art works. Museums also must ensure the safety and the comfort of their visitors, who may be disturbed by flash or trip over a tripod; in Florence the siesta hour, when visitors are few, is the only time tripods may be set up in that city's famed museums. The photographic regulations in these charts are subject to change, so it might be advisable to check with a curator in advance of any out-of-the-ordinary shooting.

A few general rules should be kept in mind. Photographing exhibits that are on loan is usually forbidden, since the items are not the museum's property. Photographing work by living artists often is not permitted, to protect the artists' rights. Photographing at a museum affiliated with a church ordinarily requires permission from the sexton, and sometimes a small donation. All in all, however, the art museum is a much more permissive place for photography than many tourist-photographers think.

United States		limitations on the use of equipment		
city	museum	hand-held camera	tripod	flash[1]
Boston	Museum of Fine Arts	no limit	forbidden	permit required
Chicago	The Art Institute of Chicago	no limit	permit required	no limit
Los Angeles	Los Angeles County Museum of Art	no limit	forbidden	no limit
New York	Metropolitan Museum of Art Museum of Modern Art	no limit no limit	forbidden weekends forbidden	forbidden weekends[2] forbidden
Pasadena	The Pasadena Art Museum	no limit[3]	forbidden	forbidden
Philadelphia	Philadelphia Museum of Art	no limit	forbidden	forbidden
San Francisco	De Young Memorial Museum Legion of Honor Museum	no limit no limit	forbidden forbidden	forbidden forbidden
San Marino	Henry E. Huntington Gallery	no limit	forbidden	forbidden
Washington, D.C.	The Corcoran Gallery of Art National Gallery of Art	no limit no limit	forbidden permit required	forbidden no limit

[1] *Only electronic flash or flash cubes may be used; open bulbs are not permitted since they may shatter.*

[2] *Flash may not be used at any time on tapestries.*

[3] *The photographer must sign an agreement that his pictures will be solely for personal or educational use, not for commercial use.*

Europe		limitations on the use of equipment		
city	**museum**	**hand-held camera**	**tripod**	**flash**[1]
Amsterdam	Rijksmuseum	no limit	forbidden	forbidden
	Stedelijk Museum	no limit	forbidden	forbidden
	Van Gogh Museum	no limit	forbidden	forbidden
Basel	Offentliche Kunstsammlung Museum	no limit	forbidden	forbidden
Brussels	Musées Royaux des Beaux Arts	no limit	forbidden	forbidden
East Berlin	Staatliche Museen zu Berlin	fee required	forbidden	forbidden
Edinburgh	National Gallery of Scotland	permit required	permit required	permit required
Florence	Galleria dell' Accademia	no limit	forbidden except 1:00-2:30 p.m.	forbidden on paintings
	Galleria degli Uffizi	no limit	forbidden except 1:00-2:30 p.m.	forbidden
	Museo del Bargello	no limit	forbidden except 1:00-2:30 p.m.	forbidden
	Palazzo Pitti	no limit	forbidden except 1:00-2:30 p.m.	forbidden
Leningrad	State Hermitage Museum	permit required	permit required	permit required
Lisbon	Museu National de Arte Antiga	forbidden	forbidden	forbidden
London	British Museum	no limit	permit required	permit required
	National Gallery	forbidden	forbidden	forbidden
	Tate Gallery	forbidden	forbidden	forbidden
Madrid	El Escorial	fee required	fee required	fee required
	El Museo del Prado	forbidden	forbidden	forbidden
Milan	Pinacoteca di Brera	no limit	permit required	forbidden
Moscow	State Pushkin Museum of Fine Arts	permit required	permit required	permit required
	State Tretyakov Gallery	permit required	permit required	permit required
Munich	Alte Pinakothek	fee required	fee required	forbidden
Oslo	Nasjonalgalleriet	no limit	permit required	no limit
Paris	Musée de Cluny	no limit	fee required	forbidden
	Musée du Jeu de Paume	no limit	fee required	forbidden
	Musée du Louvre	no limit	fee required	forbidden
	Musée de L'Orangerie	forbidden	forbidden	forbidden
Ravenna	Mausoleum Galla Placidia	fee required	fee required	fee required
Rome	Galleria Borghese	no limit	permit required	permit required
	Musei Capitolini	no limit	permit required	forbidden on paintings
	Musei Vaticani	no limit	permit required	permit required
Venice	Galleria dell' Accademia	no limit	permit required	permit required
	Peggy Guggenheim Collection	no limit	permit required	permit required
Vienna	Kunsthistorisches Museum	forbidden	forbidden	forbidden

[1] Only electronic flash or flash cubes may be used; open bulbs are not permitted since they may shatter.

Photographing Churches: A LIFE Photographer's Guide

LIFE photographer Dmitri Kessel has recorded the soaring beauty of many of the great cathedrals of the world, both for the magazine and in his book The Splendors of Christendom. In the text below and the notes on the following pages, he reveals some of the techniques he has developed in this difficult but rewarding field.

Nearly every time I take pictures of a church I approach it the way a painter approaches a still life. First I study the structure's components, noting the parts of it I like the most. Then I watch these parts of the building—a gargoyle, or an interior streaked by light from the windows—at different times of day, until I have found the most effective lighting. Only then do I start shooting.

I realize that the tourist visiting a cathedral cannot always wait for the best time of day. But he can walk around before he starts shooting. And, more important, he can watch for the detail that pleases him most; if he simply photographs that, instead of trying to encompass the entire place, he often gets a picture that serves as a better reminder than any overall view.

If the detail is inside the cathedral, remember that the time for the best illumination of the interior is an hour or two before or after noontime—i.e., when the sun is not directly over the roof. The light is then bright and angled enough to come in through the windows and bounce around.

Ordinary flash equipment is virtually useless in the dim interiors of most churches; but some color films are so fast that a good picture can be had with a time exposure of one or two seconds. To hold the camera for a time exposure in a church, a lightweight portable clamp is handy, since it can be fastened to the back of a pew.

A detail to watch for inside a church is dust in the air; the shafts of light as they illuminate the dust particles can make a more dramatic picture. And if the light rays happen to strike a fountain or a candelabra it can help fill the church's empty space.

For photographs of the whole exterior of the building, the best advice is to get as far away from the cathedral as possible, so that the picture shows both the architectural beauty of the cathedral and the way in which it dominates the surrounding buildings. Sunrise or sunset will provide the most interesting light. Many churches are also illuminated at night, some as a feature of a *son et lumière* (sound-and-light) pageant during the tourist season.

As in so many other situations where the exact amount of light is difficult to measure, the photographer shooting a church at night should bracket widely. I had this rule impressed on me once when I was photographing the floodlit cathedral at Ulm. I was exposing at f/11 for two minutes, then four minutes, then eight minutes. While I was shooting, "Pepi" Martis, the peripatetic assistant to all LIFE photographers in our Paris bureau, wandered over to watch a German tourist engaged in the same task. He came back muttering, "That guy is exposing for five minutes at f/11 in *black and white.* Why don't you try 15 minutes?" Just to please Pepi, I opened the shutter and went to a nearby café for a beer. Eighteen minutes later I returned and closed the shutter. That frame was the only one that was not hopelessly underexposed.   *Dmitri Kessel*

St. Magdalen Cathedral, Vézelay, France, 1962

This church offers a fine opportunity for the tourist because it is illuminated for a sound-and-light show almost every summer night. I chose a vantage point in a cornfield and waited until about 9 p.m., when there was just enough daylight left to present a blue background and bring out some detail in the houses. I used indoor-type color film in both a 2½ x 3½ view camera and a 35mm SLR.

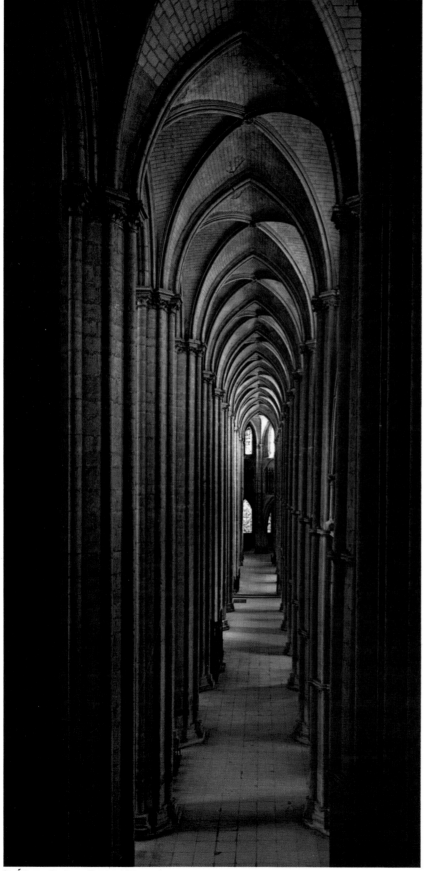

St. Étienne, Bourges, France, 1953

Here is a use of natural light, first colored by stained-glass windows, and then coloring the vaulted columns of this side aisle of the cathedral in Bourges. I solved the problem of getting a high vantage point by climbing into the choir loft. Most churches have balconies, choir lofts or similar spots from which the photographer can obtain a better perspective on the scene below.

This stairway in Wells Cathedral is bathed in ▶ natural light from the side, but I wanted also to make sure I included some of the detail above the shaded door at the top of the picture. So I had an assistant fire two flash bulbs from the doorway at right, aimed to light up the ceiling in the center. A tourist with no assistant could get the same detail by setting his camera's self-timer, ducking out of sight behind the right doorway and setting off his flash after the exposure has started.

Cathedral of St. Andrew, Wells, England, 1953

The trap to avoid in baroque churches is the scene with so many elements in it that a delight like this airborne angel gets lost in the picture. I always spend some time walking around, looking not only for what I want but also for a plain background against which to set it off. For this picture I used a 35mm camera with a 200mm lens.

Angel, Church of Our Lady, Zwiefalten, Germany, 1960

Part of the beauty of this 15th Century carving on the entrance of a pew in Ulm Cathedral —representing a sibyl, or Greek prophetess, from the legendary land Homer called Cimmeria—lies in the texture of the wood. To bring out the natural grain I used a polarizing filter to minimize the reflections and relied on natural light from the side windows. I made several long exposures at f/8, bracketing from four to eight seconds.

Cimmerian Sibyl, Ulm Cathedral, Germany, 1953

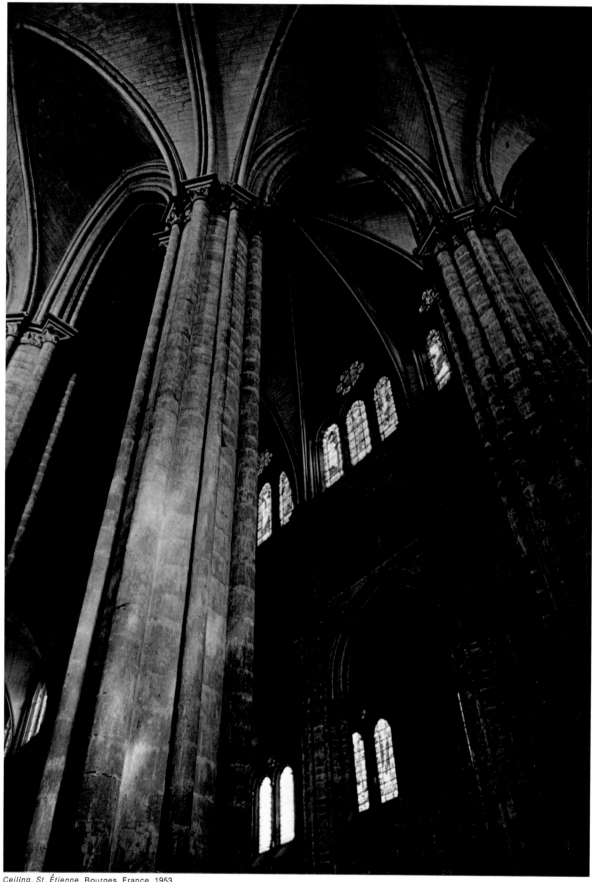

Ceiling, St. Étienne, Bourges, France, 1953

104

Any tourist can get a picture like this. All he has to do is take his camera into the cathedral, set up his tripod (after getting permission if necessary), aim at the lofty ceiling and take the exposure indicated by his light meter, letting the rays from the stained-glass windows provide the lighting. He should use an extreme wide-angle lens. I took this one at Bourges by aiming along the pillars, which the colored light turned into rainbows.

When photographing stained-glass windows it is best to concentrate on a detail rather than trying to get the whole window. Most of them are so big and so high that special equipment—a view camera or scaffolding—is needed to include the expanse without distorting some of the lines. But a detail of a window like this one can be photographed with scarcely any distortion by backing away as great a distance as the church interior will allow and using a long-focal-length lens to get a large image. For the best rendition of the design, shoot when there is no direct sunlight on the glass—an overcast day is best.

Window of the Apocalypse, St. Étienne, Bourges, France, 1953

Eve the Temptress, St. Lazarus, Autun, France, 1962

A familiar problem of lighting is the situation
in which some of the subject is better lit than the
rest of it. That's what I found in the case of this
carving of Eve in St. Lazarus Cathedral: Eve's face
and torso were nearer the window and therefore in
stronger light than the rest of the carving. I coped
with the problem by firing a small strobe onto
a sheet of white paper, bouncing the light onto the
poorly illuminated section. The same effect can
be had by bouncing a flash off a light-colored
wall, a towel or a white shirt, to provide reflected
illumination rather than harsh direct light.

Monochrome for Simplicity and Contrast 110

LENNART OLSON: *Cloverleaf in the Snow*, Stockholm, 1953

Monochrome for Simplicity and Contrast

Most tourists pack their camera bags with color film and never give a thought to black and white. Not the professionals. They know that many of the best evocations of faraway places are made in monochrome.

Color is the popular choice for most travel pictures. Yet it often is not essential to convey the photographer's intent; it may even get in the way. In some scenes the pattern, contrast between shapes, silhouettes or overall form may provide the major interest. They are better rendered in monochrome as a rule. "Black and white allows me to reach the subject immediately, without being bothered by the distraction of color," says Ikko Narahara, who made the picture at right of St. Mark's Square in Venice.

The advantage of black-and-white film for photographing such scenes is its capacity to simplify and select the essence of the view. That essence, of course, is what the human brain registers and the camera usually cannot.

How black-and-white film performs this selecting function can be seen in the picture on the preceding page. White snow, mercifully masking the ugliness of a traffic ramp in Stockholm, is marred only by the tracks of passing vehicles, and there is an esthetic contrast between the unsullied circle and the slushy border around it.

Color film, by picking up the many different hues, might have complicated the scene so that the contrast would be missed. The oil truck at top might have been an orange color, and the structure under the steps might have borne a red sign. But black-and-white film records the impression the traveler might get from his hotel window.

To make the most of the advantages of shooting travel pictures in monochrome, advance planning is necessary. An extra camera body, already loaded with black-and-white film, may come in handy. But it is not a good idea to switch back and forth between the two film types, making one shot in color, the next in black and white. The results are likely to be disappointing. Each medium requires its own approach, and the necessary mental adjustment is difficult to make repeatedly. So to some extent the challenge to the traveling photographer is to discern ahead of time the situation that may make a better picture if he takes it in black and white.

On a visit to Venice, Japanese photographer Ikko Narahara (he uses only his first name professionally) climbed a tower over St. Mark's Square to photograph this pattern of pigeons, pavement and people. He emphasized the Square's famous "crush of pigeons" with a black-and-white composition that placed the two human figures in the right foreground and the sculptured figures as a border in the background.

IKKO: *Pigeons in St. Mark's Square*, Venice, 1964

This quietly lyrical picture of the Pont-Neuf and Le Jardin du Vert Galant in the heart of Paris depends on black and white for its understated mood. Its elements—the arches rising out of their own reflections in the Seine, the spire of Ste.-Chapelle, the gray eminence of the Ministry of Justice rising from the mists in the background, and the solitary little figures on the embankment —are unified by the monochromatic treatment. They render a time and place as a study in tonal values—values that would be lost in color.

HENRI CARTIER-BRESSON: *Paris*, 1953

This stark picture of Rome's much-photographed Colosseum was taken at noon when the arches and ribs of the venerable monument stood out in sharp relief under the strong sun—their bold pattern suggesting the power of the ancient empire. The picture's inky blacks and brilliant whites have something of the harsh quality of a block print, an effect that the photographer deliberately chose to intensify by enlarging and printing his picture on high-contrast paper.

WILLIAM KLEIN: *Colosseum in Rome*, 1956

TONI SCHNEIDERS: *Stockholm Chimneys,* 1958

INGA AISTRUP: *Looking Westward*, 1960

◄ The chimneypots of Stockholm were photographed
in black and white to emphasize their strong
shapes—curiously like a row of women standing
sturdily against the background of the sky. An
orange filter helped increase the contrast between
the tones to heighten the effect of a silhouette.

On the Danish island of Fanö, where dresses like
these are still worn, Inga Aistrup photographed
a woman and children on a windswept beach.
She used black and white to get what she
calls a charcoal effect, subduing clothing colors
and emphasizing her subjects' gaze out to sea.

117

IKKO: *The Bull Ring at Ronda*, 1964

118

Shooting from a window across a narrow Spanish street, Ikko used a wide-angle lens for this picture of a man and donkey walking past the bull ring in Ronda. He chose black and white because it seemed to match the spirit of the country. Like many travelers, he "was impressed with the quality of the sun and shade in Spain. It is seen in the bright sun and black shade of the street," he says, "and also in the minds of the Spanish people."

BILL BRANDT: *London Policeman*, 1938

◀ *Seen from the dark end of a narrow London alley, a policeman stands in the shaft of light near the street. The black-and-white picture emphasizes the lines of bricks that converge on the figure, picking out his dark bobby's uniform and conveying the gloomy atmosphere of the alleyway.*

What looks like an intricate maze reveals its identity only when the eye travels to the top of the picture and discovers the people staring down on the photographer, who is shooting straight up past the rows of balconies on a La Plata apartment building. The striking pattern, strengthened by black-and-white rendition, makes the most of the massive rectangular masonry forms favored in the architecture of the city.

JORGE A. GAYOSO: *Apartment House*, La Plata, Argentina, 1965

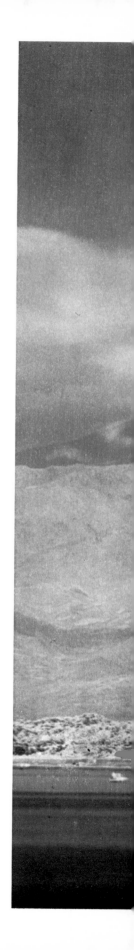

Marooned by swelling waters, like so many parts of the Netherlands, this tiny bit of land repeats its image in the quiet waterway that isolates it. In the stillness of this backwater of the delta, known as Hulst, a grove of trees stands out almost as clearly in reflection as in reality, to a large extent because the photographer chose black and white to show both as black silhouettes.

Koyo Okada, who claims to have photographed Mount Fuji 380,000 times, used infrared emulsion with an orange filter to make the great symbol of Japan seem even more awesome, towering over a Lilliputian village huddled at its base. The filter and film enabled him to cut through haze that frequently softens the view of Fuji so that in this picture the black-and-white tones are sharper than usual, making the white-capped peak stand out against the darkening sky.

AART KLEIN: *Hulst, the Netherlands, 1966*

KOYO OKADA: *Mount Fuji,* 1934

ROLOFF BENY: *Sans Souci*, Haiti, 1962

124

Riding horseback on a hillside in Haiti near the ruins of Sans Souci, the photographer noticed smoke rising from burning leaves in the valley below. He rushed down the road in time to dismount and catch this picture as a priest walked past the ancient palace, and smoke and mist shrouded the crumbling façade. Beny used an orange filter to penetrate the smoke and bring out the ghostly image of the ruins. He chose black-and-white film, he says, because "the nostalgia of time past is best expressed in black and white."

HARRY WILKS: *Scottish Bog*, 1970

Harry Wilks, who took both pictures on these pages, feels that "many of the important pictures are taken in black and white." While it may sometimes seem easier to capture a mood in color, the result may be more effective if the mood can be conveyed in black and white—particularly in this case, where Wilks wanted to record the lonely beauty of a Scottish bog on a drizzly day.

In this picture of an Italian farm, the white ribbon of road cutting across the hilly fields calls attention to the broadly rolling terrain of Tuscany. Black and white muted the colors of field and farmhouse; and printing the picture on high-contrast paper added to the stark effect.

HARRY WILKS: *Tuscan Farm,* 1968

The radiance of light pouring through a stained-glass window gives an ethereal glow to a dedication ceremony in London's Westminster Hall, inspiring a mystical mood that might have been lost if color film had recorded hues introduced by the glass. The strong white rays also outline many of the participants with contrasty backlighting so they stand out as individuals in an assembly of venerable grandeur.

BILL WARHURST: *Dedication, St. Stephen's Porch, Westminster Hall, 1952*

Making the Memorable Record of a Site 132

JULES ZALON: *City Lights,* 1971

Making the Memorable Record of a Site

Just as travelers of another generation set down their personal impressions in diaries, the 20th Century traveler uses camera and film to record the sights and sensations of his journeys. Like the diarists, he seeks more than mementos of events; for that purpose, picture postcards, ticket stubs and hotel receipts would do well enough. What he is after is images of pleasures past —pictures that depict as vividly as possible the special character of each place he visited, and that re-create the sensations he felt when he was there. His skill with the camera gives life, permanence and coherence to the potpourri of recollections and impressions he brings back home from a trip. Although his equipment is costlier and bulkier than the diarists' pen and paper, the photographer who chooses his gear wisely *(pages 78-83)* can be almost as nimble as the unencumbered diarist. And he has an overriding advantage over his predecessor: he can capture a fleeting scene with precision at the moment it occurs, instead of racking his brain at day's end to remember how things looked and how he felt.

The special personality of a place comprises complex and often elusive elements. The contours of the land, its climate and the imprints of its history and people are all part of local character. And rendering this flavor truthfully requires the painstaking observation of the diarist combined with the sensitivity of the portrait photographer: many subjects sit patiently and naturally while the photographer works to depict their faces; others mug or freeze or hide, and show their true personalities only in momentary glimpses that the photographer must be alert to capture. In the same way, some places reveal character with bold, steady directness, as the sun-drenched Portuguese beach does on page 137; others, such as the Scottish island on pages 148-149, seem to withhold the secrets of their natures until a certain time of day or a peculiar weather situation comes, when suddenly they take on an air that conveys their essence.

Like human subjects, places have many unpredictable moods, and the camera is the ideal medium for depicting both the inherent, timeless ones and the fleeting, capricious ones. Every steeple, every mountain, every village square changes constantly; no scene ever looks the same twice. A city may appear tranquil in the morning light, vital at high noon, ominous at nightfall. "What is beautiful and romantic in the mists of morning," wrote the veteran photographer-traveler Alfred Eisenstaedt, "may be completely drab and uninteresting in the middle of the afternoon—and the long shadows of sunset or the dramatic clouds of an approaching storm can turn a dull street or a flat seascape into a very exciting photograph."

Eisenstaedt himself provides an example of the changeability of local flavor in the photographs on these pages of a small church in the Lofoten Islands of northern Norway—two views of the same subject taken only a few

When Alfred Eisenstaedt photographed this Norwegian fjord at 10 a.m., the atmosphere was mild and comfortable. Faraway farms nestled into lush slopes and open sky make a cheery setting for the little church on the promontory.

At sundown, with clouds gathering, the harsh mountains stand out in profile and shadows obscure signs of life. To emphasize the sense of solitude Eisenstaedt used a long lens, eliminating the foreground crags and all but a triangle of sky.

hours apart on the same day. In one the scene, taken in the sunny light of late morning, looks crisp and cheerful; in the other, taken under gathering clouds and shadowed by the surrounding mountains, the scene is lonely and gloomy. Both versions are true expressions of the countryside of arctic Scandinavia, two of its many aspects evoking the volatile personality of this place better than just one could.

In conveying such character, time of day may make the difference, for we associate feelings with the angle of the sun and power of light—brutal at noon, gentle in evening. Yet time, as expressed by light, is only one factor that influences perception of a scene. A scent in the air, the feeling of the wind or a peculiar noise that strikes the ear—all contribute to the uniqueness of a place. With a careful choice of lens and camera angle, by composing his picture imaginatively and by focusing on certain things and excluding others from the frame altogether, the photographer can arrange a picture that suggests these subtler aspects of local color and mood. The photographer's purpose is to find and capture the visible signs of these unseen—but always essential—elements of atmosphere.

Recognizing the elements of atmosphere and synthesizing them into effective photographs require alertness and skill. In this case Eisenstaedt watched the clouds gather and guessed at the effect they would produce. Instead of heading for shelter, as a less venturesome visitor might have done, he took his chances with the dim light in order to achieve the dramatic second shot. An eye sharpened by experience had told him the picture was there, and worth waiting for. Such a clear eye is, in fact, one of the permanent rewards of traveling with a camera in hand. The habit of searching every scene for its often elusive value, and analyzing its meaningful components, makes the photographer more observant of subtleties and detail; he sees with a special acuteness that enriches every moment of the trip.

And when he returns home the same finely tuned attentiveness works as well in his own surroundings. The glittering diamonds-on-velvet view of Manhattan on the preceding page was taken by a native New Yorker whose travels have yielded pictures like the one on page 146. With a traveler's eye for the mood of a place, Jules Zalon watched the city. He observed the peculiar deeper-than-royal blue that sometimes falls over it at twilight, when it sparkles with the lights of office buildings, and on a December day he assumed the tourist's role. He bought a ticket to the observation deck on the top of the Empire State Building and stationed himself there for most of a frosty afternoon. With his camera propped on the railing, he exposed a whole roll of film—out of which came a picture that characterizes one of the world's most dynamic places. That sense of place—the picture that says this could be nowhere else—is what this chapter is about. ☐

A Sense of Place
When Time of Day Makes the Point

Time, not just timing, is one of the traveling photographer's most valuable resources. It gives a marvelously flexible way to get at the essence of a place. Every hour of every season offers a different kind of light, and every place is affected by the changing light in its own particular way. By studying the subject and watching its transformation as the day progresses, a thoughtful photographer can use this shifting illumination not only to capture the obvious elements of a scene, but also to preserve the sensations he experiences when he is there.

Not that any place has just one time when it is at its best. Moscow's Red Square can be as impressive under noontime sun as it is at dawn, and the vitality of Paris may be as well conveyed by a morning market scene as by the evening traffic in the Place de la Concorde *(pages 142-143)*. Each photographer brings his own vision—and often many visions—to every place he visits, and if his pictures are successful, takes away, in a sense, something of what he has brought there.

Beyond the fancy grillwork and filmy curtains in a once-elegant old Moscow hotel, the towers of the Kremlin rise above the emptiness of Red Square. The photographer planned this shot in advance and waited for days to get it; finally early one February morning, as the sun tried vainly to burn off the haze, she saw the somber mood of the city perfectly enhanced by a heavy gray sky and smokelike billows of clouds.

INGE MORATH: *Red Square at Daybreak,* 1967

135

CONSTANTINE MANOS: *Aegean Promontory*, 1966

On the Aegean island of Skópelos off the coast
of Greece, the midday sun seems to polish
everything in sight and to chisel every edge with
shadows. The tiny figure of a man (lower left)
is dwarfed by an old Orthodox church; the
gleam of his white shirt seems almost lost
among the flecks of light that glint off the water.

BRIAN SEED: *Beach at Nazaré, 1956*

Boldly painted high-prowed dories, beached after the morning's fishing, dominate a wide-angle view of a Portuguese village, peaceful and still in the heat of the day. In a sliver of shade an old fisherman escapes the early afternoon sun; only a carefree child is active—swinging on a rope rigged on the gunwales of two boats.

Against the purple of a cloud-covered English sunset, the towers of Lincoln Cathedral stand out of an otherwise empty landscape. The vapor rising from the cooling system of a factory in the foreground serves to heighten the dreamy, end-of-day mood, and it seems suspended like a wispy curtain between camera and subject.

Six different exposures on one 35mm frame and a ▶ lot of advance planning went into this dramatic New York sunset skyline. First, using a 28mm lens, the photographer took five successive shots without moving the camera; between exposures the sky color and cloud formations shifted, creating the cumulative effect of a backdrop that seems painted with flame. Then, to exaggerate the size of the sun, he changed to a long lens —1000mm—for the final exposure. Since the many exposures could fade the colors, he held their intensity by underexposing each time by 2½ stops.

ADAM WOOLFITT: *Lincoln Cathedral,* 1963

MITCHELL FUNK: *Cityscape at Sundown*, 1971

139

STEPHEN GREEN-ARMYTAGE: *Temple of Isis at Delos,* 1965

140

Just after sunset, the lingering daylight and the radiance of an almost-full moon combine to impart deep shadows and a golden hue to the marble ruins of a Greek temple. By silhouetting it alone against barren rocks and a cloudless sky, the photographer succeeded also in capturing a sense of historical time: no traces of modern life intrude on the mood of this ancient holy place.

To village-bred Louis Molinier metropolitan Paris is still a breathtaking swirl of activity, although he has worked there for many years. He chose to convey his awe of the big city by photographing the Place de la Concorde at night from the rooftop of a nearby hotel. With his camera set on a tripod, he made an exposure 80 seconds long, transforming streams of traffic into rivers of molten ore and street lights into white-hot sparks.

LOUIS MOLINIER: *Nighttime in Paris*, 1970

Bad Weather, Good Pictures

If there is any rule about weather that governs travel photography it is: Break the old rules. Try shooting into the sun if there is a remote chance for a good picture; if dim light is all there is, shoot anyhow despite the risk of underexposure. Above all, do not let snow, rain or fog limit picturemaking. Some of the most evocative travel scenes were taken by photographers who ventured out with their equipment on days when both traveler and camera could have been safe and dry—but gathering no memories—back in the hotel room.

Bad weather often lends a mood, suggests a particular time or even enhances a composition. An overcast sky made a perfect backdrop for the picture at right, transforming the delicate hues of the flowers into a gemlike cluster of color; in blazing sunlight, they would have competed with a brightly illuminated background and would have seemed less important. It took a grim, rainy day to present the unique view of Notre Dame cathedral on page 146.

Standard devices like lens hoods and haze filters can protect lenses from the elements. But makeshift items such as raincoats, umbrellas and plastic bags can also keep water out of equipment.

Veiled in a heavy summer haze, China's Great Wall seems to ascend into the heavens. The selection of a foggy day to shoot this scene served the photographer in two ways: it suggests the wall's staggering 1,500-mile length; and it enhances the array of delicate colors of the wild-flower bouquet in the foreground.

144

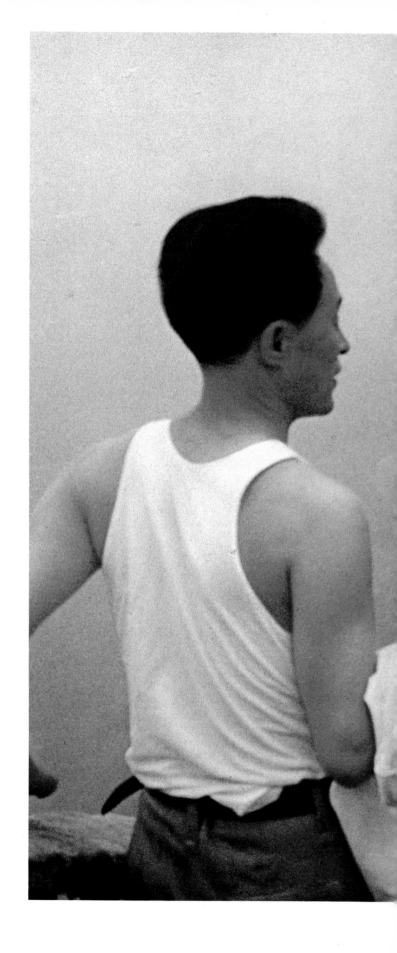

MARC RIBOUD: *Sunday on the Great Wall*, 1971

JULES ZALON: *Paris in the Rain*, 1963

On a wet day that could make the most
determined tourist want to stay in his hotel,
photographer Zalon ventured out and captured
this unique traveler's-eye view of Notre Dame.
Through the rain-splattered roof of a tour bus, he
saw a shadowy visage of the cathedral's stone
towers. A wide-angle lens' extended depth of field
kept both droplets and building in focus.

CLYDE H. SMITH: *Vermont Blizzard,* 1968

As any New Englander can testify, rural Vermont
can possess an ironic feeling of warmth even
when the temperature is below freezing and the
land is blanketed with snow. The photographer
chose to capture this comfortable sensation
by shooting during a January blizzard; the muted
red of a farmhouse and barn contrasts with the
gray sky like glowing embers on a stone hearth.

147

BILL BINZEN: *Lismore Island, Scotland*, 1971

The mood conveyed by a threatening sky, rather than the physical contours of thinly populated Lismore Island, was the objective in this picture. The North Atlantic island is only nine miles long, but the solitude a visitor feels makes it seem vast. To emphasize this sense of lonely desolation the photographer used a wide-angle lens that made the landscape surrounding his human subjects seem larger than it really was, and backlighted them against the gathering clouds that promised a sodden, blustery night.

Capturing the Unique Atmosphere

MELVIN INGBER: *Amiens, France,* 1969

Capturing in one frame the whole atmosphere of a place is an ambitious goal, yet nearly every traveling photographer sets it for himself. To achieve that aim, he must analyze his subject and his personal reaction to it, constantly asking himself, "What is it that conveys to me, here and now, the special, unique character of this place?"

At first the elements of mood may seem to defy analysis, let alone photography. Some of the most important are invisible, incapable of being recorded directly on film. Yet such qualities as warmth, desolation, antiquity, sound and smell all play crucial roles in fortifying the impact of sight. So the difficult—and yet most rewarding—task is to make a picture that connotes more of a place than the sum of its visual components. The camera can be used to translate nonpictorial attributes into a picture that stimulates more senses than vision alone.

There are standard clues that can guide the photographer in his job as mood-interpreter: reddish tones usually suggest warmth, and columns, arches and window frames are often useful devices to suggest age. But the photographer's most reliable tool is his own feeling about a place. For his personal reaction must determine how he sets his camera to render the many aspects of atmosphere in the language of color, shape, contrast and composition.

A weathered ramshackle house by a canal suggests the comfortably aged mellowness the photographer sensed in the venerable city of Amiens in northern France. The raking light of the late-afternoon sun enriches the bronze hue of cracking walls and blackens the shadows in the crevices of masonry exposed by fallen stucco.

BURT GLINN: *Spring in Siberia*, 1963

Fences marking off tracts on a collective farm
zigzag across a seemingly endless Siberian slope.
A solitary peasant woman, swathed in woolens
against the harsh wind, carries a pot of preserves,
which provides one dash of color to offset the
starkness of the landscape; otherwise, the scene
is a cold composition in black and white.

151

PATRICK THURSTON: *Albert Pub, Victoria Street,* 1967

*A long nighttime exposure, taken from the outside
looking in through etched-glass windows,
captures the warmth of a historic London pub.
Old-fashioned chandeliers, their lamp shades
slightly askew, hint at the tipsy afterglow of much
good brew and an ever-present aroma of hops.*

SHELDON COTLER: *Ljubljana Street Corner,* 1968

By shooting reflections in a convex traffic mirror at an intersection, the photographer managed to get a wide-angle view of this Yugoslavian street corner with a 135mm lens on his 35mm camera. Irregularities in the mirror surface emphasize the wobbliness of aging houses and shops.

MATTHEW MILLER: *Île de la Cité*, 1967

To portray the chaotic jumble of Paris rooftops —and avoid jostling tourists in the streets —the photographer climbed the topmost tower of Notre Dame and leaned over a parapet as far as he dared, his wife gripping his belt. The cathedral appears only in the row of sculptured stone turrets in the foreground, far below the camera's dizzying vantage point.

Against the plate-glass façade of a newly built office tower in Manhattan's financial district, Trinity Church projects a defiant symbol of 19th Century piety and elegance. The picture is a double exposure, one of many made by this Paris-based photographer to illustrate the striking modernity of the American city he often visits.

FRANCISCO HIDALGO: *Wall Street,* 1971

MARY LEATHERBEE: *A Sun-beaten Granada Hillside from the Alhambra,* 1966

A Multiple Portrait of Yosemite

HARALD SUND: *Top of Bridalveil Fall,* 1971

Although one picture can frequently sum up a traveler's feeling for a place, many travel experiences are too rich and varied to be captured in a single photograph. Some subjects are visually complex, like Disneyland or Angkor, and deserve detailed scrutiny; indeed this complexity may be what makes them tourist attractions. And sometimes a traveler's rapport with a place is so intense that only a series of images, made in the course of several visits, can properly do justice to all the moods and nuances he wants to remember after he leaves.

Two such composite portraits are exemplified on these and the following pages. The first explores the spectacular glories of Yosemite Valley through the eyes of three photographers: they approached its rocks and waterfalls not as standard tourist sights but as challenging confrontations with the natural world. (Part of the challenge is the topography of the place: its high-rising masses of stone screen out much of the light in the sky.) Taking advantage of unusual conditions of weather and time of day, capitalizing on the chance coming together of provocative visual elements, the three managed to infuse the Valley's familiar sights with new meaning. The other composite portrait, beginning on page 164, encompasses one photographer's very private feelings for the Spanish earth and the Spanish soul.

In the late-morning sun Bridalveil Fall plummets almost its full height of 620 feet in deep shadow. Only its lofty crest, torn by the wind, sparkles like crystal against a cloudless blue sky. To sharpen the contrast, the photographer underexposed—and turned the scene into an abstraction of wind and water.

HARALD SUND: *Yosemite Valley from Wawona Tunnel, 1971*

The visitor's first view of Yosemite Valley—a
sudden, breathtaking vista—is usually
photographed in daylight, but Sund chose dusk,
when meadows and cliffs lay shrouded in ghostly
silence. Working with almost no light, he exposed
his film 10 minutes and hoped for illumination
from lightning in an oncoming storm: it worked.

159

DAVID MUENCH: *Reflection of El Capitan in Merced River, 1970*

One of the most photographed rock faces in America and as integral to Yosemite as Bridalveil Fall, El Capitan is seen here afresh. The granite outcropping, twice the size of Gibraltar, is reflected upside down among snow-crusted rocks in the river far below—its size diminished but the sheer verticality of its southeast face intensified.

At the end of a wild and windy day, when ▶ Yosemite had put on an extravagant weather performance, the photographer caught the valley in another mood, one of almost Oriental quietude. The evening fog was rolling in, shrouding the rocks, softening the lines of sturdy juniper trees, fusing earth and air into one.

DAVID MUENCH: *Juniper in Fog above Tenyana Canyon,* 1970

ROBERT WALCH: *Half Dome*, 1966

Two views of Half Dome, both of them shot after sunset, combine to convey quite dissimilar aspects of the ancient rock's unrelenting granite face. In the scene above, the photographer captured a strangely ethereal quality that the harsh rock took on at nightfall. The bluish cast of his picture comes from using indoor film.

HARALD SUND: *Half Dome*, 1971

A second version, above, expresses Half Dome's
timelessness in the midst of change. Using an
extreme wide-angle lens to make the dome stand
alone in a broad landscape, the photographer
exposed for three minutes, 20 seconds—blurring
the last warm rays of the sun on a moving cloud
while the rock remained cold and immobile.

163

A Sense of Place
One Man's Spain

Increasingly, the traveler's itinerary is not 21 countries in 21 days but a close inspection of a single country or even a single area of a country. This kind of thoughtful travel enables the photographer to make a much more detailed and intimate record of the impact of a place upon his mind and eye—to sum up in a series of photographs just what makes the place special to him.

For American photographer Michael Kuh, whose pictures appear here and on the following pages, the special things about Spain are "its clear Castilian light, even better than that of Greece," its majestic landscape and its forthright people. But the traveler who proposes to capture such qualities in pictures must, in Kuh's words, "have done his homework." He must understand his subject before he shoots it, and try to sense what is going to happen before it happens. "How, for instance," Kuh asks, "can you know the decisive moment in a bullfight if you are ignorant of bullfighting?" Kuh's Spain, as it happens, has little to do with bullfights. What draws him to Spain, and what he expresses so clearly through the cumulative effect of his collection of pictures, is the lyrical quality of life in the Spanish countryside.

Along the route of the ancient pilgrimage to Santiago de Compostela in northwest Spain, the verdant open countryside looks as it must have appeared to countless thousands of pilgrims —like the promised land. The wild flowers and weeds that Kuh found at the edge of the road provide a doorstep into the medieval landscape.

A Landscape in Galicia, 1968

165

A Shepherd with His Dog, 1968

The Wine Fight, 1968

Though the Spanish peasant is generally sober and severe, sometimes he betrays another side of his nature. On a mountain near Roncesvalles (above), Kuh met a shepherd strolling with his dogs in the late-afternoon sunshine. "I liked his rugged face and the gentleness of his hand," the photographer says. At a picnic near Haro, in Spain's wine country, he was joined (above right) by a group armed with vino tinto, demonstrating, for his benefit, the village's annual "wine fight."

To Michael Kuh, his photographs of the Spanish people reveal as much about their country as his landscapes. He has lived among them for 12 years, and seeks to celebrate their self-reliance. A Spanish peasant, Kuh says, has "a self-respect, a dignity and a code of honor that I admire entirely. You cannot flip him a 1,000-peseta note and expect to push him around. 'Thank you,' he will tell you politely, 'but I have already eaten today.' " Through courtesy, an investment in time, quick thinking and occasional cunning, Kuh has succeeded in revealing the inner strength that dignifies rural Spaniards at work, at leisure and participating in the various festivals that mark the Iberian year.

A Farmer with an Umbrella, 1970

An Old Woman Mending, 1966

Gypsies at the Horse Fair, 1969

Just as a mosaic is assembled from many single tiles, so the portrait of a people can be built from individual photographs: the amused, tolerant glance of a Galician farmer (above left) peering from beneath an umbrella; the shrewd face of a gypsy trader with an elegant white Arab mare (lower left), clowning and talking with a friend at the Córdoba horse fair; and the quick look of disapproval flashed by a Spanish matron mending outside her stone house one fine day in Cuenca.

Walls of Ávila, 1969

At the Castle of the Counts of Cartagena, 1968

On every hand in Spain, the romantic past and
workaday present intermingle. Outside a noble
castle in Castile the photographer met a villager
"who had gone out there to sit, to escape his
wife's conversation." They in turn struck up a
conversation that led to a picture in which
the peasant's dignity matches that of the ruin.

◄ The medieval towers and battlements of Ávila in
central Spain, left, once guarded a great religious
seat; now the place is a provincial backwater.
Both Ávilas merge in one picture of a flock
of dusty sheep bobbing past the ancient walls.

Threshing Sledges near Frómista, 1968

"Castile in July is one golden threshing floor after another, village after village, Biblical and beautiful. This one is typical," says Kuh. When photographing people at work his credo is, "Don't speak unless spoken to; say 'buenos dias' and watch. The Spanish peasant is so secure in his world that he really doesn't care what madness you commit in yours. If it's your folly to take his picture, it's your time and film you're wasting."

Before a Holy Week Procession in Seville, 1969

Three little boys in peaked hoods and blue robes (one holding his staff upside down) await the signal to play their parts in Seville's Holy Week procession, at left. Though the occasion is one of great piety, the photograph turns away from solemnity to concentrate on the Spanish enjoyment of the pageantry of their religion.

Again, at right, the presence of a child standing behind his father among a group of barefoot penitents focuses on the human element in Seville's Holy Week celebration. The picture was made at twilight with a strobe light. Glancing off the satin robes and silver religious articles, piercing the eye slits of the hoods, the light intensifies the theatricality of the scene.

Celebrants at Twilight in Seville, 1969

To celebrate the festival of Corpus Christi, ancient Toledo displays shawls and tapestries from its windows and balconies. Below them, a procession from the cathedral wends through the narrow streets, bearing priceless works of art. Looking up, Kuh's eye was caught by the bannered design that he saw overhead —"a sunshade lit up like stained glass."

Fiesta of Corpus Christi in Toledo, 1969

174

Such Interesting People 6

LUIS VILLOTA: *Nepalese Girl at Katmandu Shrine*, 1971

The Elusive Human Element

"When she passes, each one she passes goes 'a-a-h!' " runs the song about "The Girl from Ipanema." And when he visited the beach at Ipanema in Rio de Janeiro and found that the girls were as gorgeous as the song said, Luis Villota (who took the photograph on the previous page) naturally began shooting pictures of them. Suddenly a man strode up and tried to grab the camera, accusing Villota of taking indecent photographs. Protesting that he was doing no such thing, Villota held his ground and his camera. His accuser immediately summoned two lifeguards and demanded that they confiscate the camera. At this point, Villota realized that the man was actually after his expensive Nikon, and, in halting Portuguese, he told the guards his suspicion. He convinced them and kept his camera while the would-be thief faded into the crowd.

Luckily, not many tourists will run into such a schemer if they decide to photograph the local inhabitants. And most tourists do decide to, for the spirit of a land is often revealed as clearly through the appearance of its people as through its scenery or monuments. The proof can be seen in Michael Kuh's photographs in Spain, shown in the previous chapter and in the pictures on the following pages, where facial features, attitudes, occupations or costumes mark the subjects as indigenous to their countries. National characteristics differ in fascinating ways: the religious decoration of the little shrine-goer on the previous page—kohl eye make-up, a spot of animal blood on her forehead and a flower necklace—is utterly unlike the white wedding gowns of the European brides on pages 192 and 193.

Differences in national costume are less obvious today, as old-time peasant dress becomes rarer every year; but some distinctions in clothing remain for the alert photographer to capitalize on. Official uniforms vary from country to country; no less revealing is the cut of an ordinary coat in Yugoslavia, an Italian woman's black shawl or the bowler and furled umbrella of a proper London executive. And the human being inside the clothing may provide the most emphatic national flavor of all. No one could fail to distinguish the ramrod stiffness of a British Guardsman from the casually self-confident air of an Israeli soldier.

Opportunities for photographing people characteristic of their country surround the traveler from the moment he arrives. There are peddlers in the street, traffic cops at the corners, waiters in the restaurants. It also pays to seek out public or semipublic events—carnivals, religious celebrations, even weddings—for there the camera can focus on a variety of local types all gathered to have a good time.

Since most people enjoy having their pictures taken, the tourist with a camera usually gets a good-natured response from his subjects, especially if he asks their permission before shooting. Robert Phillips *(page 182)* points out the importance of this courtesy. "Tourists who are unaware of people's sensitivities have caused so much alienation that in some countries there is a danger of more restrictions being placed on photographers."

The thoughtless curiosity of some tourists in Africa, where travelers often insist on photographing the most primitive-appearing people—not necessarily the most representative subjects—has forced at least one government there to consider desperate measures. An adviser to the tourist industry has proposed artificial villages complete with colorful but acceptably sophisticated "villagers" to pose for pictures. "It may be fake," he says, "but it's a lot less aggravation on both sides." In any part of the world it is polite—and prudent—to inquire whether local pride, custom or religious belief make people unwilling to be photographed. A guide or concierge will know.

Local custom may call for payment to someone who poses for a photographer. A tip is often expected in the American Southwest, for example, as well as in Southern Europe and many parts of Africa and Asia. If a tourist feels awkward about offering money, he can substitute cigarettes, a drink in a nearby pub, or a lift by car. There is also a growing demand for prints of the pictures in place of a tip, and providing them can be a rewarding gesture for the photographer.

Asking people to pose often produces the best pictures—even when they mug. What they do when they consciously perform for the camera reveals the way they would like to be seen. That revelation may give unusual insights into personal and national character. And when the mugging is done, the subject generally relaxes—providing a spontaneous picture that neither he nor the photographer could plan.

Candid photographs provide intimate glimpses of life and are often easier to get than posed pictures. For close-ups made without the subject's knowledge, a long lens is useful, but there are also ways to catch people unawares at close range. In a café, the photographer can pretend to be shooting the party at his own table while actually focusing on someone several tables away. Aiming the camera to the right or left of a subject may cause him to look away from the photographer to see what is being photographed. When this happens, a quick pivot with a preset camera, and the photographer has a picture with the subject none the wiser. Or a preset camera can be placed on the table and operated with a cable release or self-timer; the camera takes the picture while the photographer enjoys a glass of the local wine.

These techniques for photographing people in distant places are basically no different from ones that work at home. Only their use must change as circumstances dictate. If the photographer's attitude is open, frank and friendly, all barriers will come down, and he will capture on film his impression of a person, a people and a nation. □

The Diversity of Mankind

PATRICK WARD: *Family in Mexico City, 1965*

Both diversity and universality characterize the human race—and whichever trait the travel photographer chooses to emphasize when he photographs people, he will have good authority on his side. Henri Cartier-Bresson once said of his own attitude toward the people he photographs: "By no means do I believe that 'man is the same all over the world.' A Chinese and a European have no more in common than the fact that they both have a gender and they both eat and sleep!" Edward Steichen had another view: writing about the famous "Family of Man" exhibit he assembled that consisted of pictures of people from all over the world, he said it was meant to be a "mirror of the essential oneness of mankind."

The photographers who made the pictures on these and the following pages express that difference in their approach to their subjects. A few have ignored universality to seize on the unique—details of costume, setting or activity—that sets a person apart as someone who lives in a faraway place and observes "strange" customs. But most have used such local touches to develop an atmosphere that places a recognizably human reaction in a recognizably distant setting. Both the photographs on these pages are simply pictures of people; it is only their distinctive clothing or postures that set them apart as dwellers in foreign lands.

Although these barefoot subjects are curiously dressed in a mixture of handloomed Indian clothing and store-bought pants and cowboy hats, the photographer—shooting them against a neutral wall as they hurry along a Mexico City street—has sought to show them not as oddities but simply as a little family, doing what little families the world over do every day.

BETTY W. BENNETT: *Women near Udaipur, India, 1969*

Gathered for an afternoon of gossip, a group of
Indian women giggle with excitement at spotting a
stranger taking their picture. Their garments
are exotic and their positions, sitting on the
ground, are more Eastern than Western, but their
self-conscious reaction is a universal one.

ROBERT PHILLIPS: *Venezuelan Chef,* 1971

*While staying in Cata, a resort not far from
Caracas, the photographer noticed that the chef at
a beach restaurant liked to take cat naps on the
sand. One day he asked and got permission to set
up this picture of the artisan and his handiwork.
After the picture was taken, the photographer and
his subject lunched on the paella in the pan.*

STEPHEN GREEN-ARMYTAGE: *Greek Priests*, 1965

Struck by the color contrast between the black-garbed priests and the whitewashed houses on the Greek island of Andros, the photographer took this picture when he spied five priests walking down a narrow street, their billowing robes and high-crowned headgear making a patterned silhouette that is incontrovertibly Greek.

One eye barely visible beneath his burnished visor, an impassive young mounted sentry sits ramrod-stiff in the saddle, ready to move out into the changing-of-the-guard ceremony at Whitehall, in London. "The trooper knew his picture was being taken, of course," says the photographer. "People abroad sometimes do seem sensitive when we Americans photograph them as if they were oddities. To overcome this problem, I have my wife stand in front of a subject while I focus my camera. When I'm ready, my wife moves away and I can catch the subject more naturally."

Absorbed in street versions of their native sports, ▶ two boys in London's East End play offense and defense around a soccer ball, and a third takes a breather with his cricket bat. The photographer preserved their unself-conscious attitudes by keeping his distance and by pretending to chat with his wife as he shot with a 300mm lens.

JOHN DORISS: *Trooper*, London, 1965

COLIN MAHER: *East End Kids*, 1967

A plump-cheeked farm boy in the Egyptian Delta looks into the camera of veteran photographer Paul Strand for this head-on study. Strand's documentary-sociological style has produced many revealing portraits. This youngster's sturdy appearance, suggesting the better care and healthier life Egypt's fellahin gained after the 1952 revolution, gives an insight into the country.

PAUL STRAND: *Farm Boy in the Delta,* 1959

A schoolboy coxswain, attired like an 18th Century British admiral, barks orders to a flower-hatted oarsman wearing a seaman's jacket. The boys are taking part in the Procession of Boats, an annual event at Eton—and the picture catches the quintessence of upper-class England and its posh, tradition-bound boys' schools. The Procession's object is a tricky display of seamanship: all the crew members in a boat must get on their feet and sit down again without capsizing the craft.

HOMER W. SYKES: *Eton Boys,* 1971

The pose is occupational, used by cops the world over, but the costume says this could only be a Parisian flic. His attention seemingly attracted to a parking violation by the pointing statue above him, a Paris policeman tickets a car outside the Petit-Palais art museum. Famous for such candid pictures, Henri Cartier-Bresson, who took this one during a year's tour around his native France, stresses the importance of remaining unobtrusive if revealing pictures of people are to be gotten: "Approach the subject on tiptoe," he advises.

Serene against the wildly patterned background of ▶ wallpaper and cheap cotton print, two Moroccan women in their bordello quarters provide a glimpse of the people of North Africa that few photographers try to get. Even a professional like Cecil Beaton was frustrated when he first asked them to pose: the prostitutes ran behind curtains when he produced his camera. But once he had won their confidence—by offering money and sketching them—he found they "were apt to treat the job of posing in as professional a spirit as any other way they may be called upon to perform."

HENRI CARTIER-BRESSON: *Paris Policeman,* 1968-69

CECIL BEATON: *Quartier Réserve*, Tangier, Morocco, 1931

Resplendently Spanish in his traditional costume, a matador at the bull ring in Málaga gazes across a wooden barrier at his opponent, which has just been trotted out. "The battle fought in that brilliant costume," says the photographer, "is a most sordid reality, and the fighter, though he is a brave man, knows loneliness and terror." To communicate this terror, Ikko crouched in the first row of spectators and aimed at the bullfighter's back; the viewer shares the matador's fear.

IKKO: *Spanish Bullfighter*, 1962

A young Frenchman brings a Gallic air of romance to a stuffy wedding as he gives his bride a push on a swing at an inn outside Paris. The couple's carefree moment alone was stolen, the photographer noted, from an "entire afternoon with a full wedding party, which included uncles, aunts and small children of the family."

HENRI CARTIER-BRESSON: *French Newlyweds, 1938*

Standing in front of the Doric columns of a Fifth Century B.C. temple in Paestum, Italy, a bride and groom gaze into each other's eyes. The photographer, learning that it is the local custom for newlyweds to have their pictures taken at the temple, stationed himself at a distance and took this picture with a 105mm long lens, in order not to interfere with the official photographer and to make the columns look monumental.

DOUGLAS LYTTLE: *Italian Newlyweds*, 1971

In his official grand-marshal regalia, the leader of New Orleans' Olympia Brass Band struts past the camera at a parade. The Olympia is one of the last of the marching jazz bands that once played during funeral processions in the city, and whenever it parades, says the photographer, its leader "always has 10 or 15 photographers out taking his picture, so he hams it up for them."

CHRISTOPHER R. HARRIS: *Matthew "Fats" Houston,* New Orleans, 1971

His face a cheerful contradiction of the scowling mask pushed up on his head, a costumed participant in a Shinto festival at Japan's Nikko National Park waits to join a parade. Unaffected close-ups are easy to get during such ceremonial events, the photographer explains, "because people are usually much more interested in the event than they are in the photographer."

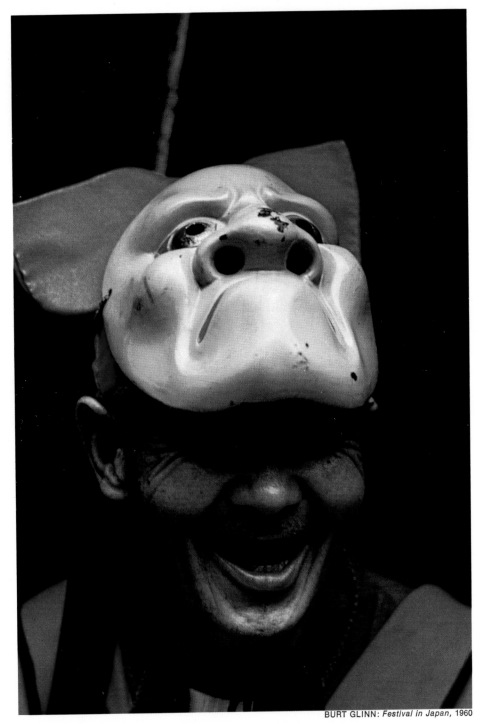

BURT GLINN: *Festival in Japan,* 1960

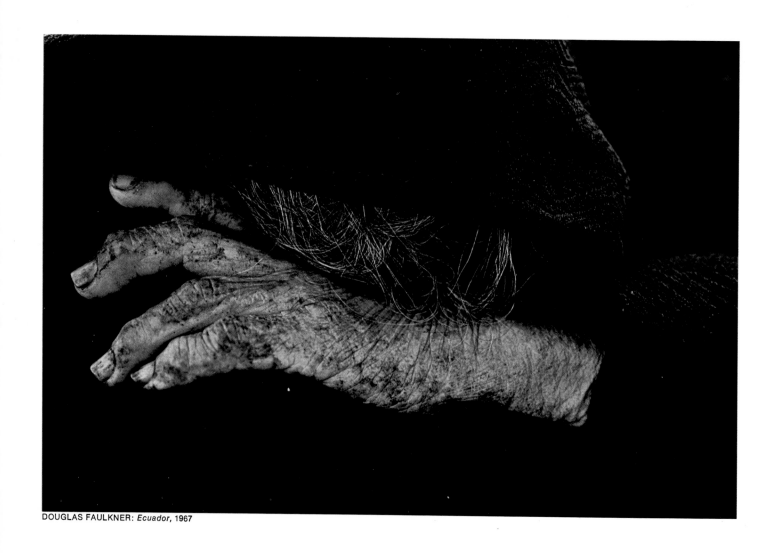

DOUGLAS FAULKNER: *Ecuador, 1967*

*The poignant detail of this close-up says as much
about the subject and her life as any full-length
portrait could. A woman's hand, coarsened by
hard work, cradles her head as she sleeps in the
marketplace of a village in Ecuador. "I had taken
other pictures of her," says Faulkner, "so
her friends didn't wake her when I took this one."*

Clichés Revisited **7**

VITTORIANO RASTELLI: *St. Peter's Square, Rome, Reflected in a 1,000mm Lens,* 1970

Escaping the Tyranny of the Familiar

Keats' lamentation "Where's the cheek that doth not fade,/Too much gazed at?" might well be applied to travel photography. Every monument and tourist attraction seems to have faded for having been too much seen and photographed. Too often the tourist himself approaches a scene with his inward eye glazed by the postcards, travel posters, matchboxes, calendars and neighbors' pictures he has had to see before. Then he photographs the place and perpetuates the cycle by producing yet another tired view—a cliché. The very word cliché entered the English language through photography; it comes from the French term that is applied to photographic negatives and other means of reproducing a single image over and over again.

And yet, professional postcard makers and amateur photographers together have not exhausted all the aspects of monuments, buildings and landscapes that have become clichés only through their photographs. Although there are no hard rules for avoiding the trite, a few hints from the experience of professional photographers can be of help. These fall into two categories. The first concerns the use of equipment; the second, the use of imagination.

Almost any extra equipment can make possible a fresh view of a stale scene. Even a clamp to hold the camera can lead to an unusual angle or suggest the advantage of a time exposure; a flash unit may provide distinctive lighting, and a prism *(pages 216-217)* converts an ordinary view into an abstraction. But probably the most useful aids are lenses of short and long focal lengths, which can make a small shift in camera position cause a tremendous alteration in the look of a scene, even when it is shot with the same lighting and from almost the same angle used by countless others.

The focal length of a lens makes a great difference in the picture partly because it influences depth of field but mainly because it controls the apparent perspective. A short lens's great depth of field is often exploited to keep a nearby object sharp while major interest is focused on the background; conversely, the long lens's limited depth can make unwanted objects in a scene so blurred they are never noticed. These effects of focal length are often overshadowed by the changes it introduces into the relative sizes and positions of objects. If the photographer backs off from his subject, a long lens can cause a distant object, perhaps slightly out of focus, to loom large and strangely close to a sharply defined one in the middle distance *(page 212);* a short lens does the opposite if the photographer moves in close—nearby objects look large and remain in focus while distant ones, just as clearly defined, appear oddly small and far away *(page 208).*

Even without extra accessories, manipulation of the camera and the film provides the photographer with room for experiment. Underexposure can silhouette a monument if its contour is more interesting than its detail. Double exposure can impart an air of mystery and symbolism *(page 209).*

More important than the use of photographic equipment is the use of imagination. Do not be hampered by the "six-foot complex," which afflicts many a photographer away from home: He stands squarely in front of every monument and shoots all his pictures from eye level, five to six feet above ground level. Every shot looks like every other one. Walking around a subject, getting close to it, stalking it like living prey, can reveal startling aspects. Viewed from beneath, the metalwork of the rather frivolous Eiffel Tower becomes a giant symbol of the industrial age. Seen from high above, the Basilica of St. Mark's takes on a fanciful, almost illusory quality.

The imaginative photographer finds ways to take advantage of possibilities others might dismiss. Stuck in a building-jammed street, he detects an unobstructed view available from the roof of a nearby hotel; a request to the hotel manager can gain him permission to make rooftop shots. In a few cases it may be possible to do something about the cliché subject itself. In Paris, the tourist has merely to ask two days in advance (and pay a reasonable fee) to get any monument lighted up at an out-of-the-ordinary time—perhaps for an unusual dawn scene. The cost of illuminating Notre Dame is about $10 an hour; the rate is higher for such monuments as the Eiffel Tower.

The free use of imagination depends on the photographer's feeling for his subject. David Douglas Duncan, who made the sparkling image of the Lido on pages 216-217, speaks of "dominating the subject." The photographer who is awed by a monument or indifferent to it is bound to produce no more than a respectful or an indifferent picture. Once the tourist is at ease with his subject, he may be able to use to advantage the accidentals of a scene, which sometimes seem to present insurmountable difficulties. Many photographers are disconcerted by the enormous traffic flow around the Arc de Triomphe. Dmitri Kessel once persuaded an agreeable "flic," who was himself an amateur photographer, to stop the traffic for him. The tourist may be hard put to do the same, but instead he can use the traffic to good effect—at night, for instance, by training his camera on the cars' headlights, recording them as colorful lines that seem to emanate from the Arc *(pages 206-207)*. The north side of the Parthenon opens into a kind of backyard rubbish heap, but the rubbish is broken masonry from the Age of Pericles and as impressive as the temple itself *(pages 218-219)*. A monument can be framed in a gateway *(page 214)* or even in a companion's camera *(page 199)*.

The photographer's ability to be mentally limber is what gives the pictures in this chapter their character, and anyone can acquire that limberness. The effort will more than repay him, for he will have achieved the highest level of travel photography. Not only can he retrace his journey again and again through his pictures, he will have the satisfaction that comes of creation, and in the end a collection that is as uniquely personal as his signature. □

The Postcard View, a Point of Departure

Picture postcards are as much a part of traveling as air tickets or passports. Introduced in 1891 by a Frenchman from Marseilles, Dominique Piazza, they now function not only as vehicles for messages to the folks at home but also as decorative exit tickets, receipts that prove one has been somewhere—and emergency substitutes for the photographic memories most travelers record with their own cameras and their own viewpoints.

As photographs, postcards present straightforward views and may capture the essence of a local mood. But the views, being standardized, are clichés, and they suffer from a propagandistic tendency to show that all is well under a heavenly, eternally blue sky. How much better the traveler might do with his own camera is indicated on the following pages, which show the same postcard scenes illustrated at right—recorded, however, by professionals who found ways to make the familiar views as fresh and exciting as they were in the beginning.

1 | St. Mark's Square, Venice
2 | Arc de Triomphe, Paris
3 | Manhattan Skyline, New York
4 | Cathedral of Notre Dame, Chartres
5 | The Leaning Tower of Pisa
6 | Angkor Wat, Cambodia
7 | Taj Mahal, India
8 | Statue of Liberty, New York
9 | Eiffel Tower, Paris
10 | Stonehenge, England
11 | Folies Bergère, Paris
12 | Mount Fuji, Japan
13 | The Parthenon, Greece

3

6

7

9

10

13

RENÉ GROEBLI: *Eiffel Tower with Sun*, 1967

204

The massive metalwork of the Eiffel Tower, a symbol of man's power, is played against a great natural power, the sun, in this forceful impressionistic photograph that was part of a series on the sun commissioned for a German concern's calendar. The photographer stood on a center divider in the Quai Branly in front of the Pont d'Iéna at noontime. He used a 2¼ x 2¼ twin-lens reflex camera and rotated it slightly during the 1/30 second exposure to suggest the turning of giant engines in the photograph.

A dazzling Arc de Triomphe seems to generate jagged lines of electricity in this picture taken during the evening rush hour in Paris' Champs Elysées. The photographer zoomed during a lengthy exposure—20 seconds. This alternation of image size with the shutter open not only thickened the streaks of headlights but also striated street lamps and the Arc itself, adding lively action to the venerable, static monument.

RON CHURCH: *Arc de Triomphe*, 1971

A bronze bell ringer and the curve of a metal support on a clock tower high above St. Mark's Square struck the photographer as being more Venetian than the lion-with-a-book or St. Mark's-with-pigeons postcard views. "The statue and the bell were floating on the city," he says. "The bell ringer seemed like a god." To achieve the floating effect in the photograph, he used an extra-wide-angle fisheye lens, which minimized and curved the background of the city beneath.

IKKO: *Where Time Had Stopped: Bell Ringer, Piazza San Marco, Venice,* 1964

This double exposure of the Statue of Liberty puts an unexpected meaning into one of the tritest symbols of travel in America. The full-length statue brandishing the torch is contained within a head that seems to be topped with a crown of thorns, while an airplane high above adds an air-age element. Both images were shot with a 200mm lens, the full-length statue slightly from the rear about half a mile away through a blue filter, and the head from about 100 yards through a red filter.

PETE TURNER: *Statue of Liberty*, 1967

BURT GLINN: *Sunrise, Mount Fuji*, 1961

A colored woodcut by the 19th Century Japanese artist Hokusai inspired this spectral view of sunrise over Mount Fuji. The photograph was taken from a Buddhist monastery on Mount Shichimen, about 20 miles to the west, a sacred spot that at certain times of the year offers a view of the sun rising right out of the crater of the dormant volcano. The photographer rose before dawn and followed the pilgrims as they went out to worship before Fuji, "The Great One."

The Cathedral of Chartres serves as a serene backdrop instead of overpowering this scene of a French farmer plowing his fields. The picture, made during the rule of Charles de Gaulle, illustrated the conflict between two moods then current in France: contentment with a secure present of neat, rich fields and longing for the majestic past. A 400mm lens made Chartres seem to loom large and directly behind the farmer.

It takes several looks to realize that this view is ▶ not the usual New York skyline and its reflection, but two identical skylines—one of them inverted. The photographer achieved this result by shooting when there was little reflection in the river. He kept the base of the Manhattan buildings across the water aligned in the center of his frame and made two separate exposures on one frame, turning his camera upside down for the second.

LOOMIS DEAN: *Chartres Seen across the Fields,* 1959

NICHOLAS FOSTER: *Brooklyn Bridge*, 1971

ROLAND AND SABRINA MICHAUD: *The Taj Mahal at Sunrise,* 1971

The Taj Mahal's great gateway gracefully frames India's most famous building and enhances its ethereal lines. The husband-and-wife team who made the photograph chose a general view instead of a detail because they felt that the beauty of the place lies not so much in the romantic Taj itself as in the harmonious combination of structures, gardens and pools.

Almost as familiar as The Leaning Tower of Pisa ▶ is the truism that "everything is relative." Both commonplaces have been put to uncommon use in this picture of an upright tower being circled by leaning Pisans and other tourists. To take the picture, the photographer simply tilted his camera until the vertical edges of the frame became almost parallel to the sides of the tower.

RALPH CRANE: *The Leaning Tower of Pisa,* 1956

DAVID DOUGLAS DUNCAN: *Le Lido,* 1963

216

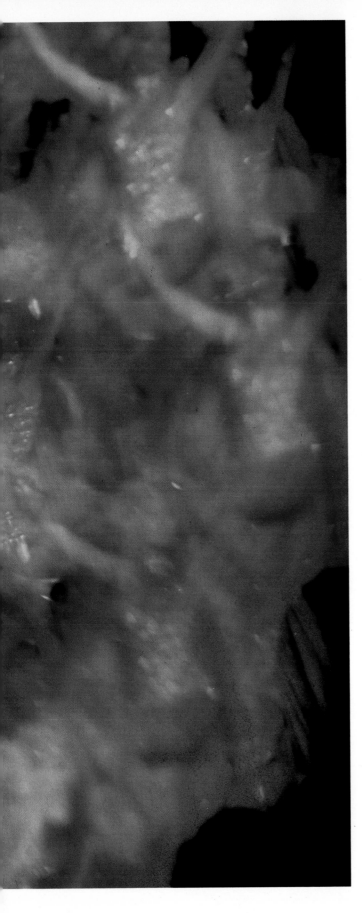

A multiple image of three Lido dancers in Paris
makes a sparkling abstraction of a subject that
could be trite—or even tasteless—treated literally.
Instead of looking stiffly posed, the dancers seem
ablaze with joie de vivre. Although this picture
was made with a five-sided truncated prism and a
multielement-lens attachment, similar effects can
be achieved with an inexpensive prism alone.

"I wanted stone to dominate," Eisenstaedt says of this unusual scene in which a massive piece of broken column dwarfs the familiar temple overlooking Athens. "I wanted to show that the Parthenon is not just an ideal of beauty standing on a lofty hill, but an actual building made of stone. It was to emphasize this sense of solidity and rock that I took the picture from a fairly low angle and included part of a stone wall."

ALFRED EISENSTAEDT: *The Acropolis*, 1964

A brilliant splash of saffron in an otherwise monochromatic setting prevents the eye from getting lost in this picture of the intricately carved ruins of Angkor. The young Buddhist priests grouped on the steps of the Bayon make up a shrewd color scheme and give a point of reference to the viewer—whose eye can then scan the rest of the monument and seek out the massive faces carved into each one of the towers. Aside from the useful color of their traditional robes, these teen-age mendicant monks add an appealing touch of life to the familiar ruins.

ELIOT ELISOFON: *The Bayon, Angkor Thom*, 1962

SONJA BULLATY AND ANGELO LOMEO: *Stonehenge*, 1971

*A sense of mystery prompted this twilight look at
Stonehenge. "Our feeling," recalls Sonja Bullaty,
"was that it transcended people and time. This
eternal cosmic quality seemed best conveyed at
dusk, with a full moon rising." The husband-
and-wife photographers stood outside the stone
circle facing east and caught the moonrise
just as the last rays of the sun lit up the stones.*

Bibliography

General

De Maré, Eric, *Photography and Architecture.* The Architectural Press, 1961.

Gernsheim, Helmut and Alison, *The History of Photography 1685-1914.* McGraw-Hill, 1969.

Jackson, Clarence S., *Picture Maker of the Old West, William H. Jackson.* Scribner's, 1947.

McCarthy, Mary:
The Stones of Florence. Harcourt, Brace, 1959.
Venice Observed. Reynal & Co., 1956.

Michener, James A., *Iberia.* Random House, 1968.

Newhall, Beaumont, *The History of Photography from 1839 to the Present Day.* The Museum of Modern Art, Doubleday, 1964.

Pollack, Peter, *The Picture History of Photography.* Harry N. Abrams, 1958.

Simon, Kate, *Italy, The Places In Between.* Harper & Row, 1970.

Smith, G. E. Kidder, *The New Churches of Europe.* Holt, Rinehart and Winston, 1964.

Taft, Robert, *Photography and the American Scene.* Dover Publications, 1964.

Thomas, Hugh, and the Editors of LIFE, *Spain.* Time Inc., 1966.

Picture Books

Avedon, Richard, and Truman Capote, *Observations.* Simon and Schuster, 1959.

Bailey, David, and Peter Evans, *Goodbye Baby & Amen: A Saraband for the Sixties.* Coward-McCann, Inc.,1969.

Bavagnoli, Carlo, *Cara Parma.* Amilcare Pizzi Editore, Milan, 1961.

Beaton, Cecil:
Photobiography. Doubleday, 1951.
The Best of Beaton. Weidenfeld and Nicolson, London, 1968.
The Wandering Years. Little, Brown and Co., 1961.

Beny, Roloff, *The Thrones of Earth and Heaven.* Harry N. Abrams, 1958.

Beny, Roloff, and Rose Macaulay, *Pleasure of Ruins.* Thames and Hudson, London and New York, 1964.

Brandt, Bill, *Shadow of Light.* The Viking Press, 1966.

Brower, David, ed., *Not Man Apart: Photography of the Big Sur Coast.* With lines by Robinson Jeffers. Sierra Club, 1964.

Cartier-Bresson, Henri:
The Decisive Moment. Simon and Schuster, 1952.
The Europeans. Simon and Schuster, in collaboration with Éditions Verve, Paris, 1955.
Photographs by Henri Cartier-Bresson. Grossman Publishers, 1963.

Cartier-Bresson, Henri, and François Nourissier, *Cartier-Bresson's France.* A Studio Book, The Viking Press, 1970.

Conrad, Barnaby, *San Francisco: A Profile with Pictures.* A Studio Book, The Viking Press, 1959.

Davidson, Bruce, *East 100th Street.* Harvard University Press, 1970.

Duncan, David Douglas, *Yankee Nomad.* Holt, Rinehart and Winston, 1966.

Eisenstaedt, Alfred:
Witness to Our Time. The Viking Press, 1966.
Witness to Nature. The Viking Press, 1971.

Freed, Leonard, *Black in White America.* Grossman Publishers, 1967.

Groebli, René, and Arthur Niggli, *Variation 2.* Visual Communications Books, Hastings House, Publishers, 1971.

Hillier, J., *Hokusai: Paintings, Drawings, and Woodcuts.* Phaidon Publishers Inc., Garden City Books, 1955.

Hürlimann, Martin, and Count Oxenstierna, *Scandinavia.* The Viking Press, 1963.

Kessel, Dmitri, and André Peyre, *Splendors of Christendom.* Edita, Lausanne, 1964.

Kirstein, Lincoln, and Beaumont Newhall, *Henri Cartier-Bresson.* The Museum of Modern Art, 1947.

Klasing, Rudolf, *Souvenir Deutschland.* Bucher-Verlag, Wabern, 1971.

Klein, William, *Rome: The City and Its People.* A Studio Book, The Viking Press, 1960.

Kruckenhauser, S., *Heritage of Beauty: Architecture and Sculpture in Austria.* C. A. Watts & Co., Ltd., London, 1965.

Lyons, Nathan, *Photography in the Twentieth Century.* Horizon Press, in collaboration with George Eastman House, Rochester, 1967.

Les Merveilles du Monde. With a Preface by Jean Cocteau. Collection Réalités, Librairie Hachette et Société d'Études et de Publications Économiques, Paris, 1957.

Meyer, Werner, ed., *Schönes Bayern.* Volume 12 of series *Deutschland im Bild.* Wolfgang Weidlich, Frankfurt am Main, 1964.

Narahara, Ikko:
España, Gran Tarde. Kyuryudo, Tokyo, 1969.
Where Time Has Stopped. Kazima, Tokyo, 1967.

Plowden, David, *The Hand of Man in America.* Smithsonian Institution Press, 1971.

Porter, Eliot, *The Place No One Knew: Glen Canyon on the Colorado.* Sierra Club, 1963.

Pritchett, V. S., with photographs by Evelyn Hofer, *London Perceived.* Harcourt, Brace & World, Inc., 1962.

Rotkin, Charles E., *Europe An Aerial Close-up.* J. B. Lippincott Company, 1962.

Schneiders, Toni, *Sweden.* Hill and Wang, 1960.

Stock, Dennis, *California Trip.* Grossman Publishers, 1970.

Strand, Paul, and Basil Davidson, *Tir a Mhurain, Outer Hebrides.* An Aperture Book, Grossman Publishers, 1968.

Van der Post, Laurens, with photos by Burt Glinn, *A Portrait of Japan.* William Morrow and Company, Inc., 1968.

Willemsen, C. A., and D. Odenthal, *Apulia, Imperial Splendor in Southern Italy.* Frederick A. Praeger, Publishers, 1959.

Guides

Adams, Virginia and Ansel, *Illustrated Guide to Yosemite.* Sierra Club, 1963.

Boulanger, Robert, *Greece.* In series, *Hachette World Guides.* Hachette, Paris, 1964.

The Editors of Holiday:
Italy. Random House, 1968.
Spain. Random House, 1964.

Guide Michelin:
Espagne. Pneu Michelin, Service de Tourisme, Paris, 1967.
France. Pneu Michelin, Service de Tourisme, Paris, 1969.
Italy. Dickens Press, London, 1964.

*Scharff, Robert, ed., and the National Park Service, *Yellowstone and Grand Teton National Parks.* David McKay Company, Inc., 1966.

Tourist Industry Bureau of Japan, eds., *Japan: The Official Guide.* Japanese Travel Bureau, Publishers, Tokyo, 1963.

Periodicals

Camera. C. J. Bucher Ltd., Lucerne, Switzerland.

Du. Conzett & Huber, Zurich, Switzerland.

Epoca. Arnoldo Mondadori Editore, Milan, Italy.

Travel and Leisure. U.S. Camera Publishing Corporation, New York.

*Available in paperback

Acknowledgments

For help in the preparation of this volume, the editors thank Gianni Corbellini, A. Mondadori Editore, Milan; Arnold H. Crane, Chicago; Fritz Gruber, Director of Photokina, Cologne; Ann McCabe, George Eastman House, Rochester, New York; the Right Rev. Msgr. Charles J. McManus, Pastor, St. Bernard's Church, White Plains, New York; M. Woodbridge Williams, National Park Service, Dickerson, Maryland. The quotation on page 178 is from "The Girl from Ipanema" *(Garota de Ipanema),* music by Antonio Carlos Jobim, English words by Norman Gimbel, original words by Vinicius de Moraes. © Copyright 1963 by Antonio Carlos Jobim and Vinicius de Moraes, Brazil. Sole selling agent Duchess Music Corporation, 445 Park Avenue, New York, New York, for all English-speaking countries. Used by permission. All rights reserved.

Picture Credits

Credits from left to right are separated by semicolons, from top to bottom by dashes.

COVER: René Groebli; Alfred Eisenstaedt.

Chapter 1: 11—Carl Mydans. 19—Jules Zalon. 20 —Patrick Thurston. 21—Bill Binzen. 22—John Doriss. 23—L. Robert Tschirky. 25, 26—Dan Budnik © 1969, from Woodfin Camp and Associates. 26—Eliot Elisofon for LIFE. 27 —Marjorie Harley. 28, 29—Patrick Ward. 30—Mary Leatherbee. 31—Jadwiga Irena Daniec. 32 —Rhoda Sidney. 33—Gregory Shuker. 34 —Maitland A. Edey.

Chapter 2: 37—Photographer unknown, courtesy George Eastman House. Pages 41 through 51 except pages 46 through 49 are copied by Paulus Leeser, courtesy Arnold H. Crane Collection. 41 —Photographer unknown. 42, 43—Alfred Stieglitz. 44—Maxime Du Camp. 45—Francis Frith. 46, 47 —Alfred Stieglitz, courtesy George Eastman House. 48, 49—William Henry Jackson, courtesy George Eastman House. 50—Félix Bonfils. 51 —Auguste Salzmann. 52, 53—Bisson Frères, courtesy George Eastman House. 54—Arthur Feldman, courtesy Arizona Historical Society Library. 55—Edward S. Curtis, courtesy The Pierpont Morgan Library. 56—Photographer unknown, copied by Paulus Leeser, courtesy Arnold H. Crane Collection. 57—Ernst Höltzer, courtesy his heirs. 58, 59—John Thomson, copied by Paulus Leeser, courtesy Arnold H. Crane Collection. 61—Fred Church, courtesy George Eastman House. 62—Underwood and Underwood —Keystone, courtesy John A. Hamlin. 63 —Keystone—Underwood and Underwood, courtesy John A. Hamlin. 64, 65—Photographer unknown, courtesy George Eastman House; photographer unknown, copied by Paulus Leeser, courtesy Arnold H. Crane Collection. 66—Paul Martin, courtesy Gernsheim Collection, Humanities Research Center, The University of Texas at Austin. 67—Paul Martin, copied by Bill

Jay, courtesy Ernest Martin Collection. 68 —Photographer unknown, courtesy Denver Public Library, Western Collection. 69—G. Lekegian, copied by Paulus Leeser, courtesy Arnold H. Crane Collection. 70, 71—Photographer unknown, courtesy Gernsheim Collection, Humanities Research Center, The University of Texas at Austin. 72—Photographer unknown, copied by Paulus Leeser, courtesy Arnold H. Crane Collection.

Chapter 3: 75—Ed Edwin. 79, 80—Al Freni. 81 —Ken Kay. 82, 83—Terence Spencer. 88—Alfred Eisenstaedt for LIFE. 89—© Lennart Olson/TIO. 90—Victor Landweber. 91—Mary Leatherbee. 92, 93—William Garnett for LIFE. 94, 95—J. P. Porter. 99—Dmitri Kessel. 100 through 105—Dmitri Kessel for LIFE. 106—Dmitri Kessel.

Chapter 4: 109—© Lennart Olson/TIO. 110, 111 —Ikko © 1972. 112, 113—Henri Cartier-Bresson from Magnum. 114, 115—William Klein. 116—Toni Schneiders. 117—© Inga Aistrup. 118, 119—Ikko © 1972. 120—Bill Brandt. 121—Jorge A. Gayoso. 122 —© Aart Klein. 123—Koyo Okada, © Orion Press. 124, 125—Roloff Beny. 126, 127—Harry Wilks. 128 —Bill Warhurst, © *The Times*, London.

Chapter 5: 131—Jules Zalon. 132, 133—Alfred Eisenstaedt. 134, 135—Inge Morath from Magnum. 136—Constantine Manos from Magnum. 137 —Brian Seed. 138—Adam Woolfitt from Susan Griggs Agency. 139—Mitchell Funk. 140, 141 —Stephen Green-Armytage. 142, 143—Louis Molinier. 144, 145—Marc Riboud from Magnum. 146—Jules Zalon. 147—Clyde H. Smith. 148, 149 —Bill Binzen. 150—Mel Ingber. 151—Burt Glinn from Magnum. 152—Patrick Thurston. 153 —Sheldon Cotler. 154—Matthew Miller. 155—© Francisco Hidalgo. 156, 157—Mary Leatherbee. 158, 159—Harald Sund. 160, 161—David Muench.

162—Robert Walch. 163—Harald Sund. 164 through 174—Michael Kuh from Rapho Guillumette.

Chapter 6: 177—Luis Villota. 180—Patrick Ward. 181—Betty W. Bennett. 182—Robert Phillips. 183 —Stephen Green-Armytage. 184—John Doriss. 185 —Colin Maher. 186—Paul Strand. 187—Homer W. Sykes. 188—Henri Cartier-Bresson from Magnum. 189—© Cecil Beaton. 190, 191—Ikko © 1972. 192 —Henri Cartier-Bresson from Magnum. 193—© Douglas Lyttle. 194—Christopher R. Harris. 195 —Burt Glinn from Magnum. 196—Douglas Faulkner.

Chapter 7: 199—Vittoriano Rastelli. 202, 203—St. Mark's Square: P. Marzari, Schio; Arc de Triomphe: Cliché C.A.P.-Albert Monier, by arrangement with S.P.A.D.E.M. 1972, by French Reproduction Rights, Inc.; Manhattan skyline: Ewing Galloway; Chartres Cathedral: Editions d'Art Yvon, by arrangement with S.P.A.D.E.M. 1972, by French Reproduction Rights, Inc.; Tower of Pisa: P. Marzari, Schio; Angkor Wat: no credit; Taj Mahal: no credit; Statue of Liberty: Ewing Galloway; Eiffel Tower: Cliché C.A.P.-Albert Monier, by arrangement with S.P.A.D.E.M. 1972, by French Reproduction Rights, Inc.; Stonehenge: British Crown copyright reproduced with permission of the Controller of Her Britannic Majesty's Stationery Office; Folies Bergère: Loomis Dean for LIFE; Mount Fuji: no credit; Parthenon: P. Marzari, Schio. 204, 205—René Groebli. 206, 207—Ron Church. 208—Ikko © 1972. 209—Pete Turner. 210, 211—Burt Glinn from Magnum. 212—Loomis Dean for LIFE. 213 —Nicholas Foster. 214—Roland and Sabrina Michaud from Rapho Guillumette. 215—Ralph Crane for LIFE. 216, 217—David Douglas Duncan. 218, 219—Alfred Eisenstaedt. 220, 221—Eliot Elisofon for LIFE. 222—Sonja Bullaty and Angelo Lomeo from Rapho Guillumette.

INDEX
Numerals in italics indicate a photograph, painting or drawing of the subject mentioned.

227

Printed in U.S.A.